THE RUNNER'S FOOT GUIDE

FEET, SHOES, MYTHS AND TIPS

ALEKS
BARUKSOPULO

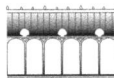

LONGUEVILLE
MEDIA

LONGUEVILLE

MEDIA

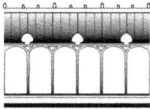

First published 2020 for Aleks Baruksopulo
by
Longueville Media Pty Ltd
PO Box 205 Haberfield
NSW 2045 Australia
www.longmedia.com.au
info@longmedia.com.au
T. 0410 519 685

Cover design: nina nielsen
Illustrations: Rosemary Fitzpatrick
Photography: Jim Fitzpatrick
International foot/leg model: Fernanda Baruksopulo

Disclaimer: The material in this book is provided for informational
purposes only and presents opinions or practices that may vary
between experts. You should consult your medical practitioner
for advice that relates specifically to your situation. The author
has made every effort to ensure that the information in this
book was correct at the time of printing and may not be
held responsible for any loss, damage, or disruption caused
by errors or omissions, whether such errors or omissions
result from negligence, accident, or any other cause.

ISBN: 978-0-6489736-1-4

A catalogue record for this
book is available from the
National Library of Australia

"The Runner's Foot Guide: feet, shoes, myths and tips is a valuable source of information for runners. Prevention 'rather than cure' is often the best course of action. Consistency in your running will enable you to be the best you can be. To allow consistency to take place it is important to look at the whole running picture when trying to prevent injuries especially whilst addressing feet and shoes."

– Pat Carroll
4-time winner of the Gold Coast Marathon,
Queensland, Australia

Pat is an Australian running legend and coach.
He is available for 'onland and online' running coaching.

For more information visit www.patcarroll.com.au or
contact him directly via pat@patcarroll.com.au

To my wife, Fernanda – thank you for being a wonderful mother, wife and person as well as helping me follow my passion.

To my children, Georgia, Elouise, and Gabriel – you inspire me every day and remember to always follow your passions.

Contents

The Author

It is interesting to reflect on how your previous sporting experiences can impact your whole life.

I know this was true for me because sport, particularly basketball, was such a big part of my young life. All I thought and dreamt about was becoming a professional basketballer. Even though this did not eventuate the dedication and effort that was put into this passion over those years, I know has influenced every part of my life since then. I was fortunate enough to have been afforded this experience and will be forever grateful to my parents for their support as I desperately tried to follow my first real passion.

Becoming a podiatrist in my mid-20s I know I was influenced by these experiences with basketball. I knew I wanted to work somewhere in sports medicine but at the time I was not one hundred per cent sure why. It was not until my early-30s that I started to figure out why I was drawn to it. Although I had many positive experiences playing basketball it was ultimately chronic injuries that lead me to give up. This was definitely heart-breaking, and it still lingers to this day. I now know this is why I am drawn to helping other injured athletes – to help them hopefully avoid the heartbreak of having to give up something they loved, as I had. Now, I find there is nothing more professionally rewarding than being able to help someone achieve their sporting goals.

The passion of helping recreational runners came a little further into my career and has evolved into my niche area of podiatry practice on Queensland's Gold Coast. Personal experiences with recreational running and triathlons, working alongside running health professionals, having the experience of previously owning a running shoe store, and constantly being around runners, helped fuel this passion.

And that's where this book comes in. As an extension of my daily work, I hope that it will reach a wider audience and help as many runners as possible enjoy injury-free running.

Although at times challenging, without question completing this book has been rewarding and I have been fortunate to be able to continue to follow this passion.

Aleks lives on the Gold Coast, Australia, with his wife and three children. He works across several locations and is best located for appointments at www.sportsmedpodiatry.com.au

He is also available for Telehealth or Video Conference consultations and can be contacted via:

✉ aleks@sportsmedpodiatry.com.au
◎ goldcoastrunningpodiatrist

Qualifications
- Bachelor of Science in the field of biomedical science, University of Queensland, Brisbane, Australia (2001)
- Bachelor of Health Science (Podiatry), Queensland University of Technology, Brisbane, Australia (2006)

Accreditations
- Athletics Australia recreational running coach (level 2)

Professional memberships
- Sports Medicine Australia (SMA)
- Australasian Academy of Podiatric Sports Medicine (AAPSM)
- Queensland Athletics – Coaching

Main professional experience
- Working in physiotherapy and sports medicine clinics since 2006, he has completed 30,000+ consults in this setting and treated recreational, semi-professional, and professional athletes.
- Previously co-owning a podiatry running shoe store in Brisbane – The Podiatry Shoe Lab.
- Previously clinical supervisor (podiatry) at Southern Cross University, Queensland

Introduction

We run for various reasons: for fun, for health, to destress, for competition, and/or because the act, in concept, is simple. Out the door and just go.

One of the main goals of a runner should be staying injury free. This enables you to continue to enjoy your running, run frequently, and continually improve – whether that be in terms of distance or time, or whatever happens to be your goal. Achieving this can be a challenge because the chance of suffering an injury while running is high. It is estimated that 50% of runners experience a running injury on an annual basis and 25% of runners are injured at any given time.[1]

Decreasing this high risk of injury is thus a major priority. As a runner, how would you go about reducing your risk of injury? To start, you need to understand the risk factors, and then you need to put in place measures to address these risks. Sounds simple, right?

Unfortunately, it seems that, even amongst professionals, there is no clear understanding of the risk factors of running injuries.[2] One of the main reasons for this is that running injuries are often multifactorial with a combination of factors unique to each individual.[3] This makes it difficult to know definitively where to focus your energy, time, and hard-earned cash. It is also difficult to obtain strong supporting evidence across the research due to differing study methodologies, populations, and even definitions of what constitutes a 'running injury'.[4]

The only risk factor that seems to have been consistently found to have strong supporting evidence is a history of prior running injuries.[5] Examples of other commonly identified risk factors, albeit with less supporting evidence, include, higher weekly training frequency, high impact forces, hard running surfaces, older age, greater weight, inexperience, leg length difference, lower leg malalignment[6], and flatter feet[7].

Many runners are often confused about the role of feet and running shoes within the running picture, including issues relating to injury prevention and performance improvement. As a podiatrist with a special interest in helping recreational runners, a previous running shoe store owner, and as a presenter at various running workshops over the years, the frequently asked questions I hear include:

1. Can you fix flat feet?
2. Is pronation bad for you?
3. Is forefoot striking better for preventing injuries?
4. Is heel striking bad for you?
5. Is forefoot striking better for performance?
6. Which is the best category of running shoe (traditional, minimalist, or maximalist) for preventing running injuries?
7. Which is the best category of running shoe (traditional, minimalist, or maximalist) for performance?
8. Which is the best running shoe brand?

One of the inspirations for writing this book was to answer these frequently asked questions and, by doing so, to bust some common running myths. Where possible, I have tried to make the answers clear and easy to understand, offering such supporting evidence as is available and where appropriate. I also provide general information about feet and running shoes that I hope will clarify the important role they play in the overall running picture.

Using this knowledge, you will be better able to assess information you come across in various forms of media. I hope this book will also help you to make more informed decisions about choosing a course of injury prevention and/or seeking face-to-face advice from a podiatrist or other health professional about treatment including helping you to make the best decisions about what shoes you run in.

A final inspiration for this book was my desire to pass on running foot tips that have helped my patients over the years. These tips can be used to complement your overall injury prevention plan. As you will come to understand, there is unfortunately no magic bullet (or magic shoe!) when it comes to preventing running injuries. Instead, we need to look at the whole running picture and cover as many aspects of injury prevention as possible in order to help decrease your risk.

How best to use *The Runner's Foot Guide*

My goal is to be as informative as possible about all aspects pertaining to the feet and running shoes. I have not attempted to write a running guide that covers topics that lie outside my area of expertise. In saying this, as a podiatrist working with runners and sports clients, we are still trained to assess the overall running picture as well as being aware of most injury-contributing factors. Once we identify other factors, we know when it is necessary to work as part of a team, incorporating other health and medical professionals for the best patient care. I make mention of these situations throughout the book.

Finally, this book is not intended to replace face-to-face advice and treatment from a suitably experienced podiatrist or other health professional, especially if you are currently injured. Instead, if used as a source of reference, the information in this book should complement helping you not only to prevent injuries but to enjoy your running even more.

Section 1 | Feet

*'The human foot is a masterpiece of engineering
and a work of art.'*

– Leonardo da Vinci

Although it can be argued that feet are an odd-looking part of the body, with some people even being offended by them, in my opinion, Leonardo's quote is a great description. The ways in which all the bits and pieces of the foot coalesce to function, provide good reason for us to be in awe of the overall design of the human body.

The foot's main role is to transmit loads between the lower leg and the ground. An inability to do this effectively, especially during activities such as running (during which such loads are large and repetitive), can result in an overload of the musculoskeletal system.[8] Without the foot's unique design, we wouldn't be able to keep our body upright, absorb impact forces, or adapt to the different surfaces upon which we move. Indeed, it has been suggested that this unique design, which allowed for bipedalism (using only two legs for walking), was instrumental in setting humanity on a different evolutionary path from our closest neighbours.[9]

This section covers basic foot anatomy, with appendix 1 offering more detail about the musculoskeletal structures of the foot. Foot types and arch heights are also explained. How the foot functions during the gait cycle is discussed including the role of pronation and supination. Finally, the different running foot strike patterns are examined.

Frequently asked questions I address in this section include:

1. Can you fix flat feet?
2. Is pronation bad for you?
3. Is forefoot striking better to prevent injuries?
4. Is heel striking bad for you?
5. Is forefoot striking better for performance?

Let's start by exploring the basic anatomy of your feet.

1

Basic foot anatomy

There are 26 bones (28, if you count the regular sesamoid bones), 33 joints, and over 100 muscles, tendons and ligaments in each foot. Together, the bones in your feet comprise over a quarter of all of the bones in your body.

The bones in the feet can be divided into three main sections:
- The **forefoot** includes the 14 **phalanges** (toe bones) and corresponding five **metatarsals**.
- The **midfoot** includes the **navicular**, the three **cuneiforms** (medial, intermediate, and lateral) and the **cuboid**.
- The **rearfoot** includes the **calcaneus** (heel bone) and **talus**.

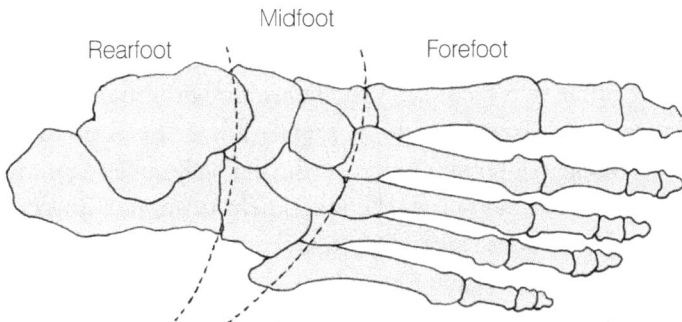

Bones and sections of the feet

The connection of two or more of these bones to each other creates the joints in the foot as well as the ankle, which is the connection to the rest of the body. Movement of the foot involves bending a number of these joints in the different planes of the motion of the body, namely the **sagittal, frontal,** and **transverse planes.**

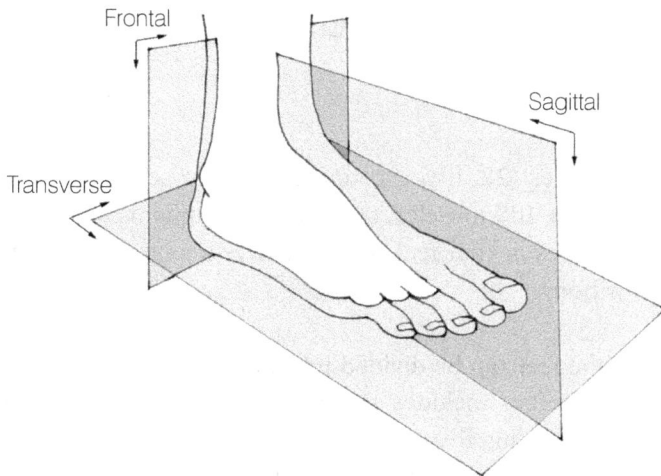

Planes of motion

There are three arches in the foot, which may surprise some people, because most only know of one, the visible **medial longitudinal arch**. The other two arches are the **lateral longitudinal arch** and the **transverse arch**. Together, these arches allow the foot to flexibly adapt to changes of terrain and load during walking and running.

Ligaments that inter-cross the joints help to support these arches and keep the bones together. In particular, the strong **plantar ligaments** (those under the foot) play a role in supporting the arches as well as engaging in a minor elastic energy return role.[10]

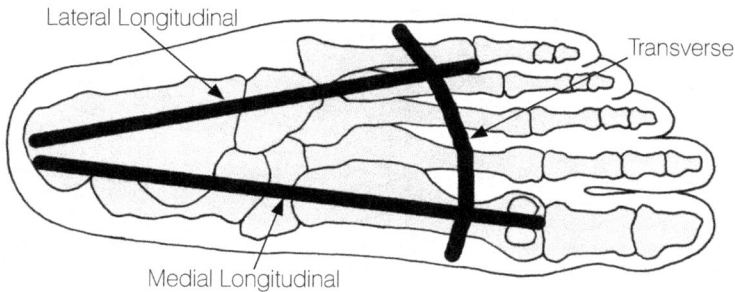

Three arches of the feet

An important medial longitudinal arch-supporting structure of the foot is the **plantar fascia**. One end is inserted into the bottom of the heel bone and the other into each of the five toes via the plantar plates. The plantar fascia has three main parts: medial, central, and lateral. The central part is commonly referred to as the **plantar aponeurosis**[11] and is the major supporting and elastic energy returning component.[12]

The position of the plantar fascia, especially in relation to the heel bone, the joints in the midfoot, and the bones of the medial longitudinal arch of the foot, create a triangular structure or truss.[13] This formation is what helps prevent the arch from separating and collapsing while weightbearing.[14] This triangular truss and the plantar fascia also play a significant role in foot function by way of the **windlass mechanism** (discussed in more detail in chapter 3).

Further structural stability for the arches is provided by the plantar **intrinsic muscles of the feet**, of which there are four layers underneath each foot. These muscles are also important for the finer motor actions of the feet; for example, flexion of the toes.

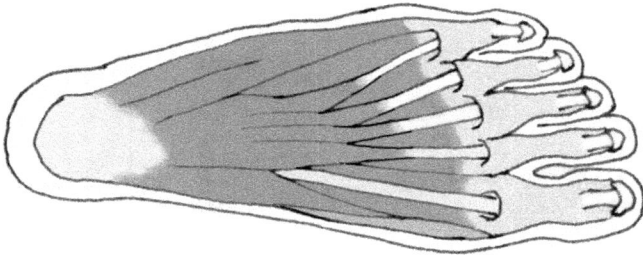

Four layers of intrinsic muscles under the foot

The arches of the foot are further supported by the **extrinsic muscles** of the feet via the tendons that cross the ankle from muscles, all but one of which originate originate in the lower leg. In addition, these extrinsic muscles help to generate movement at the ankle during the different stages of the walking and running gait cycles.

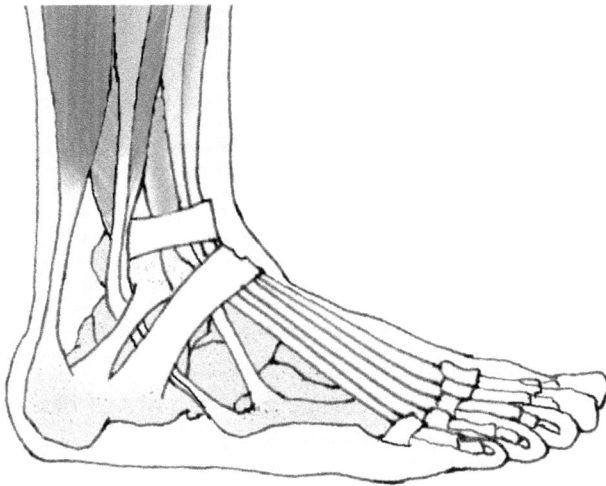

Extrinsic foot muscles and associated tendons, lateral view

More detail of the different musculoskeletal structures of the foot can be found in appendix 1. It is also a handy source of reference if you happen to sustain an injury and would like to learn a little more about the affected structure. Common running foot conditions such as Achilles tendinopathy, plantar fasciitis, and Morton's neuroma are also briefly discussed there.

2

Foot types and arch height

It is important to understand your individual foot type, particularly since there is a functional relationship between the basic arch structure of the foot and the biomechanics of the lower limb.[14]

The three basic foot types, often referred to as foot posture, are categorised in the standing position as:

1. pes cavus – a high-arched foot
2. pes planus – a low-arched or flat foot
3. neutral – a neither high- nor low-arched foot

It is the extremes of the high- and low-arched foot types that are more commonly associated with potential musculoskeletal conditions, linked purely to the natural structure of an individual's foot.[15] Although important to establish, a neutral foot type by itself does not contribute to musculoskeletal conditions. The cause of these extremes can be either congenital or acquired later in life.[16] Determining whether the joints in a runner's foot type lie outside the normal range of movement, i.e., hypomobile (rigid) or hypermobile (overly flexible), is also important, as each can place undue stress on certain anatomical structures during movement.

Assessing both the foot type and flexibility type of a runner before observing them while running may provide insight, as high arches and flat feet have each been associated with injury patterns in runners. For example, high arches have been linked to higher occurrences of ankle injuries, bony injuries, and lateral injuries. In contrast, flat-footed runners report more knee injuries, soft tissue injuries, and medial injuries.[17]

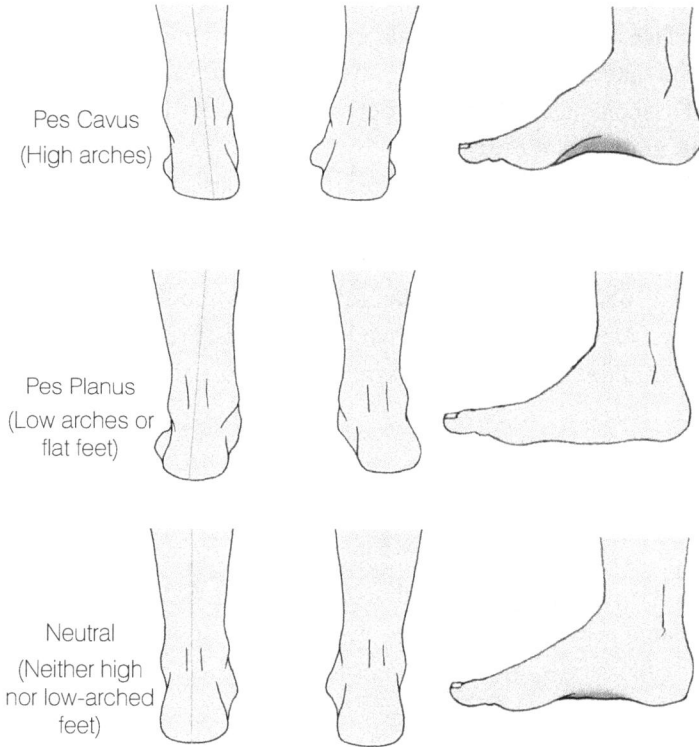

Pes Cavus
(High arches)

Pes Planus
(Low arches or
flat feet)

Neutral
(Neither high
nor low-arched
feet)

The different foot types

Pes cavus (high-arched foot type)

Pes cavus is the medical term for a high-arched foot, often associated with hypomobility (rigidity). On the higher end of the scale, this foot type may not permit adequate unlocking of the bones of the foot to allow the arch to act as an adaptor and shock absorber during foot strike. If the foot does not provide sufficient shock absorption, this can lead to increased foot and lower limb fatigue, as well as pain in the knees, hips, and lower back.[18] The greater inverted angle of the heel typically created from a very high arch can also create instability, which can lead to ankle injuries, especially on uneven running surfaces. The inverted angle can also contribute to greater work for the lateral extrinsic foot muscles (peroneal longus and brevis) and associated tendons in order to counteract the foot rolling out, leading to potential overuse.

In particular, painful symptomatic presentations and conditions associated with high arches include forefoot pain (metatarsalgia), painful forefoot callouses, pain under the sesamoid bones (sesamoiditis), plantar heel pain, lateral ankle instability, peroneal tendinopathy, Achilles tendinopathy, lower limb stress fractures, knee pain, iliotibial band friction syndrome, and osteoarthritis of the hip.[19]

Pes planus (flat-foot type)

Pes planus is the medical term that describes a flat foot and is often associated with hypermobility. As with high arches, there is a spectrum for flat feet. In most cases, especially if there is no current injury or history of associated injuries, flat feet are not something to be concerned about and do not need to be addressed.

The flatter the foot, the more likely it is to cause a disruption of the ideal functioning of the foot. For example, if the foot stays flat for too long after the heel lifts off the ground during the propulsion phase of running gait (over-pronation, see chapter 3), certain muscles and associated tendons must work harder to stabilise a looser bone arch structure as well as help move the body forward in a less efficient functional length. This extra work and load on these structures may contribute to an overuse running injury.

Painful symptomatic presentations associated with flexible flat feet include generalised lower limb pain, increased lower limb fatigue, Achilles tendinopathy, osteoarthritis, patellofemoral disorders,[20] medial tibial stress syndrome,[21] and hip pain.[22]

FAQ #1: Can you fix flat feet?

I am often asked by patients with flat feet if they can be 'fixed'. As discussed above, flat feet are a normal variation and, in many cases, especially if there is no pain, they are not something to be concerned about. To be clear, flat feet do not need to be 'fixed' just because they are flat.

For running activity, flat feet should still be identified as part of a multifactorial assessment.[23] Some injury risk associations with having flat feet have been identified, in particular, medial tibial stress syndrome and patellofemoral pain, but evidence to indicate they conclusively increase the risk of running injury by themselves is still lacking.[24]

Even if you wanted to, there is actually no way to 'fix' flat feet by permanently lifting and setting the arches higher. It is not possible to change the shape of your feet using foot orthoses. (The role of foot orthoses is discussed in appendix 2.) Likewise, foot-strength exercises do not lift or change the shape of the arch, although they can provide further support to the existing foot type or posture by not allowing the foot to deform as much.[25] Barefoot running has also been shown to strengthen the intrinsic and extrinsic muscles,[26] but it will not change the shape of the feet, despite some mis-held beliefs.

The foot posture index and identifying your foot type/posture

Runners are often unsure about what foot type they have, and when they guess, I find they are often wrong. This is where the foot posture index, or at least parts of it, may more clearly define some of the signs of your foot type/posture.

Primarily used by researchers, the foot posture index is a fast, simple method of visually classifying foot posture. It is fairly reliable and offers a criterion validity that helps standardise foot types included in research studies.[27]

The foot posture index is based on six visual foot posture criteria used to classify a foot as flat, high-arched, or neutral (neither flat or high).[28] These include:

1. Position of the head of the talus (the bone on the very top of the foot).
2. Observation of the curves above and below the lateral malleoli (the bony bump on the outside of the ankle).
3. The extent of calcaneal (heel bone) inversion (tilting out) or eversion (tilting in).
4. The extent of the bulge in the region of the talonavicular joint (located at the highest part of the medial longitudinal arch).
5. The congruence of the medial longitudinal arch.
6. The extent of abduction (away from midline of body)/adduction (towards midline of body) of the forefoot on the rearfoot.

If some of the descriptions above are confusing, the following is a simplified version to help determine what foot type/posture you have.

Please note that the following self-observation questions are merely a home exercise. They are not scientifically validated in any way, and should only be used for interest's sake and not replace a professional examination. If you want a definitive clarification on what foot type/posture you have, please consult a podiatrist.

The following self-observations are best assessed in three positions:
1. **Front-on to a mirror:**
   a) Do your feet lean toward the midline of your body? Perhaps you notice a bulging of the bump (medial malleolus) on the inside of your ankles? You may also notice no clear sign of arches, or that they are very low to the ground. If so, you may have a flatter foot type.

b) Do your feet lean or hang towards the outside of your body? Do you see very clearly defined high arches? If so, you may have a higher arched foot type.

c) Do your feet appear relatively level, not leaning to either side, and with no medial bulging of the bump inside each ankle? Do the sides (medial and lateral) of your ankles appear congruent? Are your arches discernible? If so, your foot type is probably neutral.

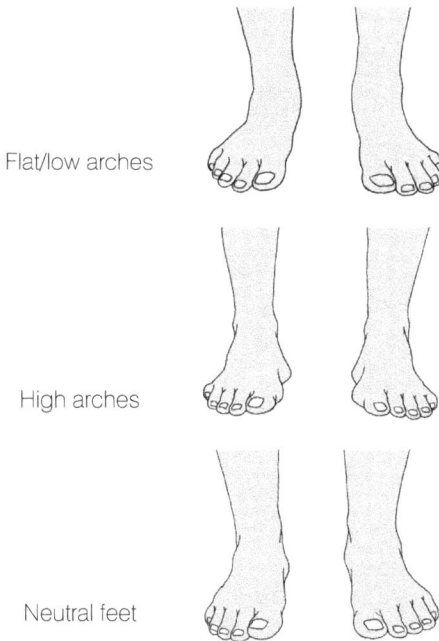

Flat/low arches

High arches

Neutral feet

Front view of feet when facing mirror

2. **Side-on to a mirror with the inside of one of your feet facing the mirror (the other foot should be behind so as to not obstruct the view; remember to swap after observing the first foot):**

a) Is your arch very close to the ground, or even dead flat, i.e., no arch at all? If so, you may have a flatter foot type.

b) Do you have a clearly defined high arch that forms an apex? If so, you may have a higher-arched foot type.

c) Does the arch appear to be clearly neither of the above, but instead a more congruent arch? If so, your foot may be neutral.

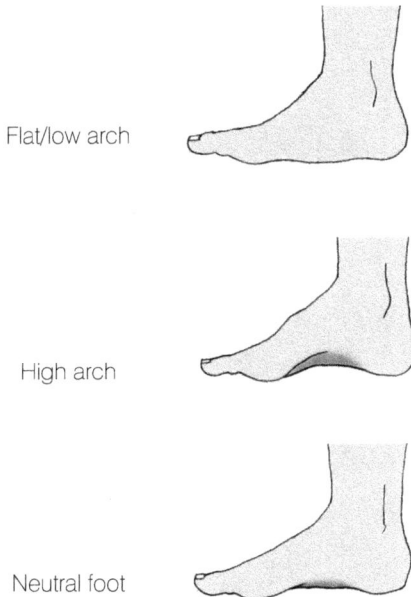

Flat/low arch

High arch

Neutral foot

Side-on view of the medial longitudinal arch, when facing mirror

3. **Take a selfie, from behind, of the back of your feet from the floor, using your phone camera's timer feature and propping the phone up:**

a) Do your heel bones lean in towards the midline of your body? Perhaps you notice a bulging of the bump on the inside of your ankles again? These may indicate a flatter foot type.

b) Do the heel bones and feet appear to lean towards the outside of your body? Do you notice outward bowing of the Achilles tendons? These may indicate a higher-arched foot type.

c) Do the heel bones and Achilles tendons appear to be straight, with no lean to either side? Do the sides (medial and lateral) of each ankle appear congruent? These may indicate a neutral foot.

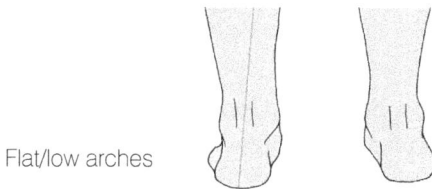

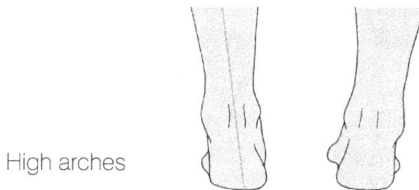

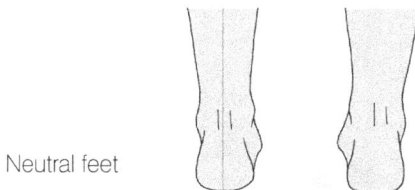

Flat/low arches

High arches

Neutral feet

Rear view of feet, as seen on camera

3

Foot function during the running gait cycle

Understanding how the foot should ideally function during the running gait cycle helps you better understand the purpose of their unique design, and why a podiatrist might intervene if they identify a potential inefficiency that may be contributing to a running injury. When describing the gait cycle, I have done so in its simplest form to illustrate the foot's functional role for the purposes of this book. As such, keep in mind there are a number of other processes that need to occur in the body for overall efficiency during the running gait cycle, ones that fall beyond the scope of this book.

The running gait cycle starts when one foot strikes the ground and continues until that foot is in the same position again.

There are two phases of the running gait cycle:

1. stance
2. swing

Two phases of the gait cycle

We are particularly interested in the stance phase, as this is where the feet play their functional roles. The **stance phase** of the running gait cycle can be further divided into three stages:

1. initial contact
2. midstance
3. propulsion

| Initial Contact | Midstance | Propulsion |

Three stages of stance phase

As discussed earlier, the foot's functional roles are shock absorption of impact forces, adaption to surfaces, and transfer of forces from the lower limb to the ground to move the body forward. Shock absorption and adaptation ideally should occur from initial contact through to early midstance. The transfer of forces to the ground for propulsion should occur during late midstance until toe-off.

There are two important foot movements that allow these functional roles to occur.

1. Pronation

Simply, this describes the foot rolling in towards the midline of the body and the arch lowering towards the ground. This movement occurs at initial contact and continues through early midstance. This movement allows the bones of the foot to become more mobile, so the foot can become a shock-absorbing, adaptable structure.

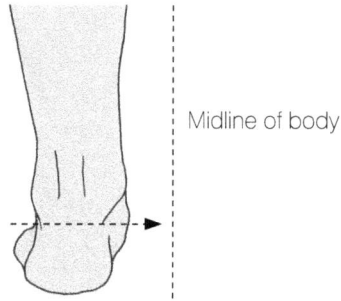

Left foot pronation – should occur from initial contact to early midstance

2. Supination

This is essentially the opposite of pronation where the foot rolls away from the midline of the body and the arch lifts. When the foot re-supinates, this positions the bones of the foot into a more 'rigid lever' for efficient transfer of forces to the ground. This should ideally occur during late midstance until toe-off.

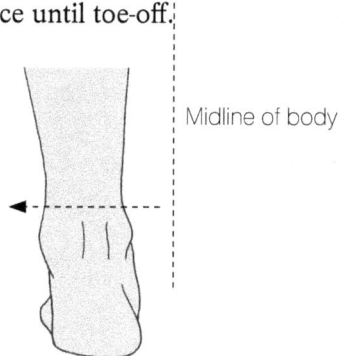

Left foot supination – should ideally occur from late midstance to toeoff

FAQ #2: Is pronation bad for you?

Pronation is required during running and plays an important role in shock absorption and adaptation, as just mentioned. It is a normal part of foot function and is not bad for you.

In the past and even to this day, pronation has often been incorrectly demonised as the root cause of many running injuries. This may have stemmed from the running shoe industry, whose once commonly used term 'anti-pronation' running shoes alarmed many runners unnecessarily about pronation for decades.

'Over-pronation' is another frequently encountered term. Linked to a flat foot type, it commonly refers to the foot continuing to pronate too far, past what is considered the ideal positioning, where the foot should start to re-supinate, i.e., from late midstance. If the foot is delayed in re-supinating, its bones are delayed in 'locking' together. This is thought to place greater stress on various soft tissue structures supporting the arch, because the foot is not as stable or efficient structurally as it should be for propulsion.

Although over-pronation is commonly identified as contributing to certain injuries, it has not consistently been found to be a risk factor for running injuries.[29] This is an important consideration if, for example, we consider intervening with foot orthoses purely to address over-pronation, especially if there is no injury. If a runner has no injury history and is not currently injured, I do not believe there is a need to improve the functioning of the feet just because a runner displays over-pronation. As long as all other areas of running injury prevention are covered, a runner can continue to run with feet that are deemed to over-pronate with no more potential injury risk than runners who do not over-pronate. As discussed in appendix 2, there is potentially a role for foot orthoses (custom or non-custom) if a runner has a related injury.

The windlass mechanism

The windlass mechanism helps to explain one way in which the bones of the feet transition from pronation to supination during late midstance. As the heel lifts off the ground, the toes simultaneously bend. This causes tensioning of the plantar fascia and a consequential lifting and shortening of the medial longitudinal arch. During running gait, this assists other foot musculoskeletal structures and body mechanisms to re-supinate the foot into the more 'rigid lever' position ready for efficient propulsion described earlier.

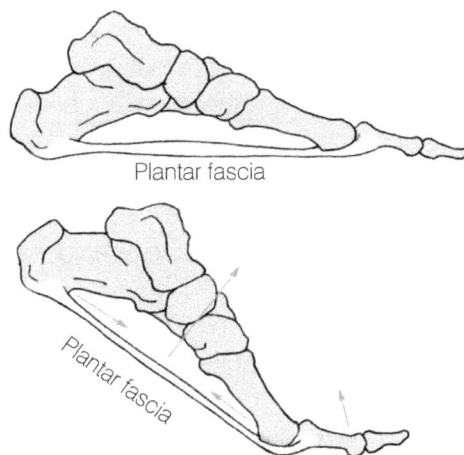

Plantar fascia

Plantar fascia

Windlass mechanism

The delay or the complete failure of this mechanism as a potential consequence of over-pronation described earlier may contribute to excessive stress on midfoot structures and the foot's muscles and tendons.[30] Assessing this mechanism and how to facilitate it more easily, if affected, is one aspect we look at as podiatrists if potentially intervening with foot orthoses.

The lower kinetic chain – how the foot affects the whole lower limb

The lower kinetic chain of the human body can be easily understood if you think about the different leg segments (foot, lower leg, upper leg, and pelvis) as connected and moving in a coordinated manner to facilitate movement. It has been described a little more definitively as a combination of several successively arranged joints contributing to a complex motor unit.[31]

I demonstrate to my running patients how the foot influences the rest of the lower limb segments while they stand in front of a mirror, a simple exercise you can do at home. This exercise also offers a simple way to understand how the feet can contribute to running injuries further up the leg.

Stand in a relaxed position, legs bared to mid-thigh, and slowly roll both feet towards the outside of your body. This movement is known as supination, as described earlier. Observe the rest of the leg segments externally rotating (limbs twisting out) to follow. Now, roll both of your feet in the opposite direction (pronation) towards your body's midline, observing what happens to the segments: the other segments follow by internally rotating (limbs twisting in).

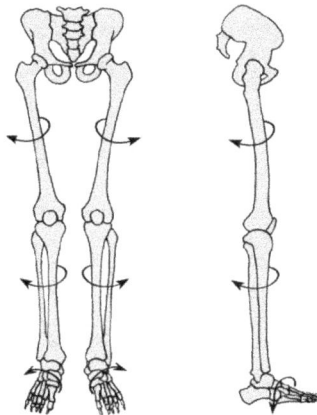

Lower kinetic chain – supination of the feet and external rotation of the limbs

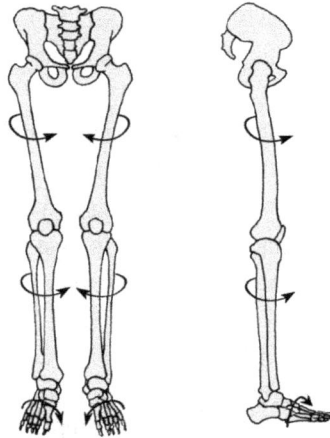

Lower kinetic chain – pronation of the feet and
internal rotation of the limbs

Relating this demonstration to movement and potentially contributing to an injury, in most cases we are looking for what was described earlier as 'over-pronation' and how quickly over-pronation may occur. If this is occurring, then soft tissue structures further up the leg potentially have to work harder to control the segments of the lower kinetic chain. This extra effort may be a contributing factor to an overuse injury.

Part of an overall treatment plan if there is a related injury may involve intervention with foot orthoses, trying to improve any identified inefficiency.

4

Foot strike patterns

It is important as a runner to understand the different foot strike patterns and the potential they have for overload and injury in relation to certain parts of your feet and lower limbs, particularly if you are thinking of changing your foot strike pattern.

The discussion about which foot strike pattern is better for you has been ongoing for a while and is still one of the most hotly debated topics in the running world today. It closely mimics the debate between the traditional running shoe (which typically promotes a heel strike) and the minimalist running shoe (typically thought to help promote a forefoot strike), discussed in chapter 7.

There are three running foot strike patterns:

1. heel strike
2. forefoot strike
3. midfoot strike

1. Heel strike

During a heel strike (also referred to as rearfoot striking) the heel lands first, followed by the forefoot. At heel strike, the ankle is dorsiflexed (foot pointing up) with the heel inverted (tilted outwards) at landing. The foot lands in front of the centre of mass, with the knee in a slightly flexed (knee bent) position. From this contact position the foot dorsiflexes (bends up) and everts (leans inwards) while the knee continues to flex. From midstance, these movements reverse until the foot leaves the ground.

Note: Heel striking does not automatically indicate overstriding or bad technique. This is discussed later in this chapter, in FAQ #4.

Heel strike

2. Forefoot strike

During a forefoot strike the heel lowers to the ground before lifting again for propulsion. Compared to heel striking, the ankle is plantar flexed (foot pointing down) during foot strike and the heel is more inverted (tilted outwards). The knee lands in a more flexed (knee bent) position with the foot placed directly below the centre of mass. Due to the plantar-flexed position and more inverted heel position, when compared to heel striking, the foot goes through more dorsiflexion and eversion range in total.[32]

Some runners may strike on their forefoot because they have severely restricted ankle joint range of movement. They may naturally shift to this position because it is more comfortable when landing on hard surfaces while going barefoot or wearing minimalist running shoes, and/or it may be how they have always run naturally.

There are many reported benefits in using this strike pattern over heel striking, which we will cover in a moment. However, it is important to note that what is sometimes referred to as 'toe striking' (where the heel never touches the ground) is a rare strike pattern amongst long distance runners and, therefore, not considered here.[33]

Forefoot strike

3. Midfoot strike

With the midfoot strike, the heel and forefoot strike simultaneously and show intermediate effects in terms of movement of the foot and lower limb in contrast to heel or forefoot striking.[34]

This strike pattern is highly variable,[35] making it hard to confirm consistently in runners. Slow motion video analysis on a treadmill can help verify this strike pattern more clearly. Viewing a runner while they are fatigued, especially during initial analysis or when seeking to identify a midfoot strike, is important. A slight variation in gait caused by fatigue may cause the midfoot striking runner to change their strike pattern to either heel or forefoot.

As the benefits of midfoot striking appear similar to those of forefoot striking,[36] these two patterns are sometimes mentioned together in research. Accordingly, the following FAQs compare heel striking with forefoot striking.

Midfoot strike

FAQ #3: Is forefoot striking better for preventing injuries?

Despite much discussion there is no conclusive evidence that one strike pattern is better than another for reducing the overall risk of injury.[37]

The most common scenario when a runner is looking to change their strike pattern is a heel striker intent on becoming a forefoot striker.

So why is forefoot striking often promoted over heel striking?

This is due to the altered positions at the ankle and knee (described earlier) and therefore the change of load applied to the body. Basically during forefoot striking more load is placed and absorbed by the soft tissue structures of the ankle and foot.

In particular this has the effect of creating no impact transient (burst of energy or force) at strike and is thus associated with vertical loading rates that are approximately half those of heel striking.[38] This is due to the greater bending of the ankle and eversion (tilting inwards) of the foot where soft tissue structures such as the Achilles tendon, tibialis posterior, and plantar fascia can now lengthen to absorb the impact forces.[39] This has been suggested as potentially beneficial in the prevention of running-related injuries.[40] In particular, a high-impact transient is thought to contribute to tibial stress fractures and plantar fasciitis.[41]

Despite the clear mechanical benefits that are touted by researchers, the debate over forefoot striking continues. One suggestion for this is that possibly only a few studies have examined the relationship between strike pattern and injury.[42] A second reason cited is that current evidence is limited to retrospective findings (as opposed to prospective findings), which have fewer potential sources of bias.[43]

So, if you are not currently injured, there is no apparent benefit in changing your strike pattern solely to prevent injuries. If you do decide, however, to change your strike pattern without careful consideration and guidance, you could potentially open yourself up to an increase in load in other areas, which may lead to increased risk of a running injury.[44]

Different foot strike patterns may, however, predispose runners to different types of running injuries.[45] Below are examples of commonly associated lower limb running injuries for heel and forefoot striking, as well as the proposed reasons for such associations. You will notice plantar fasciitis is mentioned for both patterns, for different reasons.

Table 1

Heel strike	**Tibial stress fractures** – due to impact forces[46]
	Plantar fasciitis – due to impact forces[47]
	Patellofemoral pain – due to impact loading and longer stride length[48]
	Anterior lower leg chronic exertional compartment syndrome – due to the dorsiflexed ankle position at foot strike[49]
Forefoot strike	**Plantar fasciitis** – due to the increase in load as well as fatigue of the intrinsic foot muscles[50] which are less able to play their supportive role
	Achilles tendinopathy – due to increase in both load and recruitment of the calf and Achilles tendon[51]
	Metatarsal bone stress fractures – increase in load as well as fatigue of weak intrinsic foot muscles,[52] which are less able to support these long bones

---

FAQ #4: Is heel striking bad for you?

Heel striking is often demonised because it is mistakenly viewed as being the same as overstriding. Keep in mind that overstriding can only occur during heel striking and is a commonly identified technique flaw which increases impact forces and may increase the risk of injury.[53] One reason why runners may overstride is that some beginners and novices believe that to run faster, they need to take longer or larger strides. Others may unknowingly overstride even if they are a little more experienced. This overstriding causes the runner's feet to strike too far out in front of their body's centre of mass, placing increased decelerating impact forces back into the body.

Heel striking itself is not bad for you. You can still run with great technique and reduced impact forces when you heel strike. The preferred way to prevent overstriding, instead of changing your strike pattern, is to increase your running cadence.[54]

How to increase your cadence – if required

Cadence is the total number of steps you take per minute. A high cadence shortens your stride, enabling your foot to land closer to your body's centre of mass. Research indicates that even a 10% decrease in stride length, while still heel striking, results in a significant impact load reduction on the hip and knee.[55]

In terms of cadence, 90 steps per minute (spm) for a single foot, or 180 total spm for both, is commonly identified (and debated) by experts as ideal[56] to elicit the aforementioned effect. It should be noted that if you are significantly lower than this (more than 20% lower, for example), trying to increase your cadence by such a large amount from your usual step rate may prove challenging to adopt and actually compromise performance.[57] For example, it has been shown that greater oxygen consumption is required when step rate increases by more than 10% of preferred rate, whereas increases less than or equal to 10% of preferred rate reveal minimal change to metabolic cost.[58]

If you do not know your current cadence, it is definitely worth tracking and taking this factor into consideration. Ways to do this include using a running watch that has real-time cadence, where you can also check your average at the end of your run. If you run with a less sophisticated watch, you can count the number of steps you take on one foot over a 20-second period and then multiply by three to get the total number of steps you take on each foot per minute.

If your running cadence is significantly lower than 180 spm in total for both feet and you want to increase it safely, remember first of all not to do so by more than 10% to make it easier to adapt to. You can use real-time monitoring via a smart watch, as mentioned, or a metronome running app which ticks over at the desired beats per minute (bpm), allowing you to match your steps to the beat. Alternatively, you can do the same by listening to songs that have the desired (or at least close to) bpm. A quick search of your favourite music app will reveal a number of desired bpm running songs and playlists.

If you have trouble increasing your running cadence, especially, for example, if you are still more than 15–20% below the recommended 180 spm for both feet, I suggest consulting a professional who can help you. Other technique flaws that fall outside of the scope of this book may be affecting your ability to run with a higher cadence. An experienced running health professional may also determine that your current cadence is acceptable and not something to change, depending on your technique, experience, goals, and injury history.

An exception for changing your strike pattern

There may be situations where a running health professional might look to change or suggest an alteration to a running patient's strike pattern, such as where persistent injuries occur that may be linked to a particular strike pattern. If a change is made, it needs to be done carefully, with guidance as well as a clear understanding by the practitioner and runner as to what other areas may be impacted (see table 1, page 28).

One example of when we might change a forefoot strike pattern to a heel strike pattern is where a beginner or novice runner has persistent, recurring pain in their Achilles tendon and/or has not responded to conventional rehabilitation protocols. Even though some studies suggest that forefoot striking can lead to stronger calf muscles and Achilles tendons,[59] too much load too soon, without the appropriate conditioning, can lead to an overuse injury of this structure. Heel striking places less load through the Achilles tendon, so part of the overall treatment plan might include changing their pattern to a heel strike to help lessen the load on the calf and Achilles tendon.[60] Making this change would, importantly, include keeping an eye on the runner's cadence to make sure they are not overstriding and closely monitoring them for any symptoms in certain musculoskeletal structures that are loaded more with heel striking. The appropriate core and lower limb strengthening program would need to be in place, especially with greater load now being placed on the knees. A change in the runner's training program would also need to be made to accommodate learning and adapting to the new strike pattern as well as the altered loads placed on different parts of the lower limbs.

FAQ #5: Is forefoot striking better for performance?

A common belief held amongst some recreational long distance runners is that to run faster, you need to forefoot strike. The reason most commonly given is that when we strike on our forefoot, we can better tap into the stored energy of our body's natural springs, in particular the Achilles tendons and the foot's plantar ligaments.

To better understand this reasoning, the Achilles tendon, the largest and most elastic tendon in the body, reportedly returns around 95% of the elastic strain energy stored with the loads typically encountered during running.[61] The longitudinal and transverse arches of the feet, which include many elastic structures such as the plantar fascia and other plantar arch ligaments, recover an estimated 6–17% of the mechanical energy generated on each step.[62] During a heel strike pattern, these structures do not stretch on impact; stretching only occurs approximately when the forefoot has contacted the ground, which means that the full advantage of this elastic energy mechanism is not available.

Nevertheless, it is very important to understand that despite tapping into these natural springs while long distance running, any running economy gains may be offset by higher contractile costs of the calf muscles and the intrinsic foot muscles.[63] That is, these muscles will fatigue faster.

Being able to strike on your heels and still run fast can be best demonstrated by knowing what the fastest long distance runners in the world do in terms of foot striking. I must admit at the beginning of my podiatry career I, too, incorrectly believed that because elite runners move so fast, they must all strike on their forefoot. This, however, is not the case, as shown in one study that assessed the strike patterns of elite international runners at various stages of a half marathon. For example, at the 15 km mark, they found that 75% of the runners used a heel strike, 23% a midfoot strike, and only 2% used a forefoot strike.[64] Apart from being able to run very fast while striking on their heels, these athletes wouldn't continue to strike on their heels if it significantly contributed to persistent running injuries that would prevent them from training. They simply would not be able to do the high mileage, at the required intensity, to enable them to compete at such a high level.

Interestingly, the higher percentage of heel strikers amongst the elite running population is comparative to that in studies of recreational runners. One study that compared foot strike patterns of 286 recreational runners in a marathon found that at the 10 km mark, 88.9% of runners struck on their heels, 3.4% struck on their mid-foot, 1.8% struck on their forefoot and 5.9% of runners exhibited discrete foot strike asymmetry.[65] There was also no significant relationship between foot strike patterns and race times.[66]

Section 2 | Running shoes

Shoes enable us to walk or run on different terrains and explore on foot as we desire. Without them, we would be more limited in our ability to get out and about, and even to function on a day-to-day basis. So much of our daily life revolves around standing, walking, and exercising on unnatural, hard, and unforgiving surfaces. We need shoes to protect our skin and cushion our bodies.

Historically, running shoes were designed to help improve performance. Over the centuries, athletes have experimented with various forms of running sandals, hoping to gain an advantage during running events. For example, the ancient Etruscans attached the soles of sandals to the upper part with metal tacks, while the Romans used tongs to wrap the shoe as closely to the foot as possible to maximise traction.[67]

Fast forward to our modern-day running shoe design (whose origins are in the early 1970s). Their various features are designed to help prevent running injuries and improve performance. The goal of features such as cushioned gels and composite foams is to dampen high-impact forces, which have been linked to increased injury risk.[68] Features such as dual-density midsoles, stability wave plates, and guidance rails all aim to alter motion to improve functioning of the feet, especially if there is over-pronation, commonly identified as a risk factor for a running injury despite the lack of strong evidence.[69] Lastly, features such as energy-returning midsoles, carbon fibre plates, lightweight foams, and lightweight one-piece woven uppers are geared to improve running performance. For example, lighter running shoes are often linked with enhanced running performance by improving running economy.[70] (On the controversial inclusion of carbon fibre plates into running shoes for the purpose of improving performance, see chapter 7.)

In this section, we examine the basic anatomy of the running shoe and include brief analyses of some features designed to prevent running injuries and improve performance, as well as exploring the different types of running shoes within the traditional and non-traditional categories.

Frequently asked questions addressed in this section include:

1. Which is the best category of running shoe (traditional, minimalist, or maximalist) for preventing running injuries?
2. Which is the best category of running shoe (traditional, minimalist, or maximalist) for performance?
3. Which is the best running shoe brand?

5

Basic running shoe anatomy

Understanding the anatomy of running shoes can reveal the level of thought that has gone into the design, especially how particular pieces are positioned and come together to function, and what may be of particular importance for your unique foot shape, type, and/or function.

Last

The last of a running shoe determines the shape of the shoe, the width of the toe box, the depth of the toe region, the toe spring (the upward curve of the shoe at the forefoot), and heel height.

There is some question as to whether running shoe brands still employ various last shapes (see below) within their range versus only changing the shape and dimensions of the midsoles. Regardless, the following information will give you an idea of the thought behind the design of the last's shape.

The three main types of last shapes are curved, straight, and semi-curved. A curved last has a C-shape and is generally the lightest of the three and deemed the least supportive. This type of last is typically found in traditional high-mileage neutral shoes, traditional lightweight trainers, and traditional racing flats (see chapter 6 for further description of these). A straight-lasted shoe typically includes traditional high-mileage maximum-stability shoes and is the most supportive, albeit the heaviest of the three. A semi-curved last shape is found in the majority of running shoes which balances being moderately supportive while not as heavy as straight-lasted running shoes.[71] Traditional high-mileage moderate-stability shoes are an example that have semi-curved lasts. Keep in mind that there are variations with the shoe categories that use different last shapes.

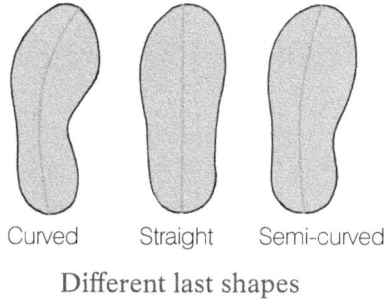

Curved   Straight   Semi-curved

Different last shapes

Running shoes can be broken into two main sections, each with important components.

1. Upper
   a) heel counter
   b) quarter/quarter panel
   c) heel tab
   d) heel collar
   e) vamp
   f) toe box
   g) tongue
   h) laces
   i) eyelets

2. Bottom
   j) midsole
   k) outersole
   l) shank
   m) insole (*inside of shoe not shown on diagram*)

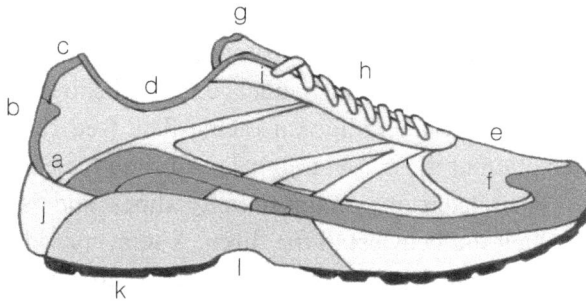

Anatomy of a running shoe

1. Upper

The upper is the top part of the shoe that encloses and holds the foot in the shoe. Whether certain components are included or not, as well as the materials that are used, varies between brands and models within brands. The evolution and selection of materials usually revolves around trying to make the shoe as light as possible for performance while still providing an accommodating, supportive, breathable, durable shell. An example of a more recent advancement is the one-piece woven seamless upper, aimed at making shoes lighter, more comfortable, and supportive.

Explanation of upper components:

a) **Heel counter** – the plastic insert that curves around the back of the heel. It provides rigidity to stabilise the rearfoot. Whether this feature actually does increase rearfoot stability and should be a staple in certain shoes is questionable, especially as removing the plastic heel counter reduces the weight of running shoes.

b) **Quarter/quarter panel** – covers the heel at the back and sides.

c) **Heel tab** – the notch at the back of the shoe designed to protect the Achilles tendon and lock the heel comfortably into the heel counter.

d) **Heel collar** – an extension of the heel tab which wraps around the ankle (under the malleoli, or ankle bumps) to further hold the rearfoot comfortably within the shoe.

e) **Vamp** – the upper section from the toes extending back towards the quarter.

f) **Toe box** – the very front section of the shoe; also, the area inside the front of the shoe.

g) **Tongue** – permits the foot to slide more easily into the shoe and protects the top of the foot from lace pressure.

h) **Laces** – locks the feet into the shoes. There are several ways to lace your shoes that provide either added support or offload certain areas. (See section 3, tip #2, for a discussion of some of these.)

i) **Eyelets** – through which the laces are threaded.

2. Bottom

j) Midsole

The main purpose of the midsole is to provide cushioning from impact forces and provide energy return during propulsion. The foot function type the shoe has been designed for determines whether a stability feature is built into the medial part of the midsole. Traditionally referred to as medial posting, these features are designed to decrease the inherent instability of cushioned midsole foams and control the amount and/or rate of over-pronation. Each brand has their own proprietary design features that at least attempt to achieve this. (See chapter 6 for more information on stability running shoes.)

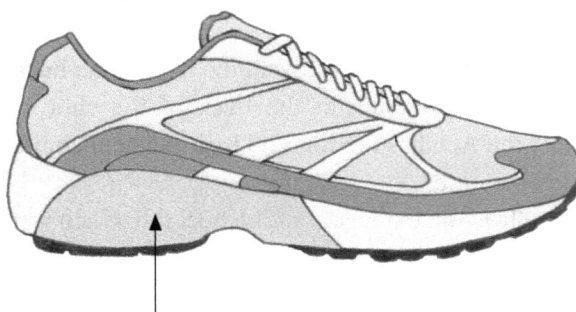

Example of dual density feature

The stack heights of the midsole refers to how thick the midsole layer is at the heel and forefoot. An example of standard stack heights in a traditional high-mileage cushioned running shoe is 22-mm at the heel and 12-mm at the forefoot. This difference between the heel and the forefoot stack height is called the heel drop, heel pitch, or heel offset. In the above example, the difference is

10-mm, which is a common differential for traditional running shoes. Each shoe brand, and even models within brands, can have varying stack heights and heel drops, depending on what the shoe has been designed for and the brand's belief about how their shoes affect biomechanics, the mechanics of movement. Stack heights and heel drops also help define minimalist and maximalist running shoes (see chapter 7, non-traditional running shoes).

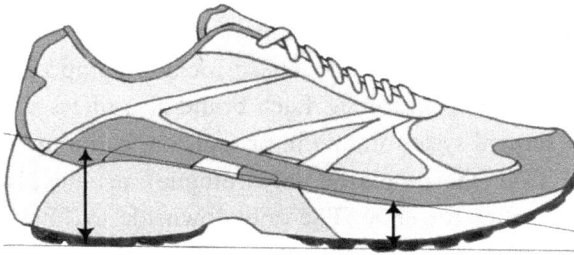

Heel drop

One reason why an elevated, thicker-foamed heel section was originally built into traditional running shoes was to provide greater dampening of the high-impact forces that occur while heel striking. Another was to lessen the load on the calf muscles and Achilles tendon by shortening them. Despite being a feature since the inception of traditional running shoes, there is conflicting evidence on whether or not an elevated heel yields such desired effects and helps decrease the risk of running injuries. For example, since the introduction of an elevated heel in traditional running shoes, records of Achilles injuries have increased, not decreased.[72] Overall injury rates have also not changed since the inception of the modern running shoe design in the 1970s.[73] Keep in mind that there are conflicting reasons given for this lack of change in injury rates, including, importantly, that runner demographics have changed.[74] (See chapter 7, FAQ #6 for other possible reasons for an absence of change in injury rates.)

The most common material used for the midsole of running shoes is a foam-based material called EVA, ethylene vinyl acetate. Not only is it cheap to make but it is relatively light. It also has a density that is soft enough to provide adequate cushioning from impact forces, yet firm enough to provide a certain durability and responsiveness during propulsion.

The area and part of the gait cycle in which the shoe makes initial contact with the ground also determines where each brand places their proprietary technology in the midsole. For example, each brand has different heel strike cushioning or impact dampening systems. These include composite foams to help dampen impact forces. Each brand also offers some kind of 'energy return' system to aid in propulsion, commonly a blended form of TPU (thermoplastic polyurethane), usually placed at the mid to front of the shoe. The only downside to TPU is that it is heavier, which is why it is not commonly used as the main midsole material. (See chapter 7, FAQ #7, for information about the more recent use of a lightweight, highly responsive, advanced version of foam called Pebax. How the controversial carbon fibre plate also fits into the equation to help performance is discussed.)

k) Outersole

The outersole is the base, or underside, of a running shoe and is usually made of carbon rubber and/or blown rubber, both designed to protect the softer midsole layer while providing traction.

Carbon rubber is the tougher of the two. If these two rubbers are used in combination under the same running shoe, carbon rubber is usually placed at the heel of a running shoe for more durability from initial contact wear. Carbon rubber is the preferred go-to rubber for the outersole of trail running shoes and helps prevent wear on rougher terrains. Blown rubber, which is lighter and softer, and offers a little more cushioning, is predominantly used in road-running shoes.

Both forms of rubber are more rigid and stiffer than the softer midsole foam above them, making them more durable, better able to withstand scuffing on initial contact and provide protection from wear and perforation by stones and other sharp objects on trails. Without this protective layer, the midsole foam would wear out very quickly.

The rubber also provides traction in the form of lugs, the size and pattern of which is determined by what terrain the shoes are designed for. For example, trail running shoes often have larger lugs to gain better hold on softer dirt, grass, and gravel surfaces. For purely road running, such aggressive traction is not needed. In addition, larger lugs can make shoes stiffer on impact and therefore less comfortable for running on roads.

l) **Shank**

The shank is a supportive structure designed to provide further bend and torsional stiffness in the midsole. If included, when looking at the shoe from the side, it is located in the centre of the midsole. The structural design varies amongst brands and models. The category of running shoe can dictate whether this component is included. For example, minimalist running shoes do not traditionally include shanks because they don't want to interfere with the natural movement of the feet. Many traditional running shoe models appear to be moving away from including shanks for the same reason. Excluding the shank also makes the running shoe lighter.

m) **Insole**

Also termed a sock liner or innersole, the insole is the first layer of foam or cushioning beneath the foot. It absorbs perspiration and helps absorb impact forces. Terry cloth lining is often used to help absorb perspiration, while EVA is commonly used to help with impact forces.[75]

Another important function of an insole is to prevent the foot from slipping inside the shoe, reducing the potential for blisters under the foot as well as those caused by the foot rubbing against the outersole's interior.[76] Most insoles are removable, which is useful if they need to be replaced with a more cushioned version or non-custom or custom foot orthoses. It also makes it easier to dry and air out the shoes after use or washing.

In regard to foot orthoses, please refer to appendix 2 for more information on how they are proposed to work and the role they play in the overall running picture. It is important to read because as a runner you will inevitably come across foot orthoses, whether you see them in a running shoe store or are prescribed them by a podiatrist to help with a running injury.

6

Traditional running shoes

The word 'traditional' describes the type of running shoe design that has been used in the mainstream running community since the 1970s. Its features are designed to inhibit running injuries and improve performance. Although advances in technology have improved various elements of the traditional running shoe, the basic shape, design, and many features remain the same.

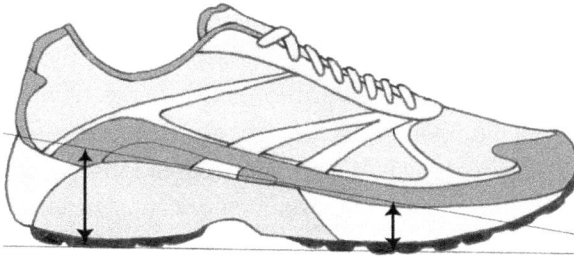

Traditional shoe design showing an
elevated heel defining a traditional shoe

The following are four types of traditional running shoes:

1. **High-mileage** – These shoes tend to have a greater midsole stack height in both the heel and forefoot in comparison to the other types of traditional running shoes. This allows room for cushioning and stability features which also make them heavier. Other defining features of this type of running shoe include a 10–12-mm heel pitch, depending on the brand. Some models may offer a slightly lower heel pitch, such as 8-mm, which means

they could also be also classed as a minimalist running shoe, as you will read later. As the name suggests, this type of traditional shoe is typically used as the main training shoe for longer-distance training sessions. On average, you can expect to get between 600 and 800 km of road running from this shoe, although this figure can vary between individuals, brands, and depends on the type of foams used in the midsole. With technological advances in materials, the overall weight of this type of shoe appears to be decreasing; however, a typical high-mileage cushioned running shoe can still weigh 300+ grams per shoe for an average-sized men's shoe. For example, the Asics Kayano 26 sits at 314 grams for a men's size US 9 and 272 grams for a women's size US 8.

2. **Lightweight trainer** – This shoe is not as cushioned or supportive by design as the high-mileage cushioned running shoes discussed above. Because of the reduced cushioning and therefore firmer feel underfoot, this type of running shoe often feels faster and more responsive. It is typically used for shorter, lower-mileage training sessions, including intervals, tempo, and speed sessions. It is also used as a race-day shoe by many recreational runners. There can be stability or motion control features (e.g., dual-density foam midsoles) built into this traditional running shoe type. However, because of the overall lower midsole stack height, these are often minimal and, in my experience, it is questionable whether they are even worth being included. The stiffness of the midsole, in terms of torsion and where the shoe bends, will vary between brands and models. Motion control and stability features also tend to be heavier, and their inclusion in this type of shoe will defeat its purpose as a lightweight shoe. Stripping away features to make this shoe lighter typically reduces its longevity. Observationally, I have found 400–600 km is the average life span of this type of running shoe, if running purely on roads. The overall weight will also vary depending on the brand, size, and whether it is for a man or woman. These shoes commonly weigh 200–300 grams. For

example, the Brooks Launch 5 are 261 grams for men's size US 9 and 224 grams for women's size US 8.

3. **Racing and performance shoes** – When speed is the goal, the shoe needs to be as light as possible, although ideally not compromising on comfort and stiffness, as you will learn later. Traditionally, this shoe has a very small stacked cushioned midsole, with minimal to no heel pitch and no stability features. Keep in mind this trend of small stack height for racing and performance shoes has more recently changed to maximum yet lightweight stack height with the advent of Nike Vaporfly and Alphafly (see chapter 7, FAQ #7). Used for races or events, this shoe does not have a long life expectancy. I find on average they last between 300 and 400 km when used for road racing, perhaps less depending on the runner and the brand's model. This shoe typically weighs between 150 and 250 grams, depending on brand, size, and whether it is for a man or woman. For example, the Adidas Adizero Adios 4 weighs 221 grams for the men's size US 9 and 193 grams for the women's size US 8.

4. **Trail shoes** – There are specific trail-only shoes as well as hybrid versions that can be used for a mix of road and trail running. Most traditional trail running shoes have similar midsole features to road running shoes, with the main differences being in the outersoles and uppers. The outersoles have tougher carbon rubber, different tread patterns, and larger lugs, aimed at the better traction needed for trail running. The upper material can feature water protection, drainage, and areas of tougher protection against environment factors. Depending on the terrain for which the shoes are designed, midsole stability features may not be included, because having a little more flexibility can sometimes be beneficial on trail runs. You can expect trail shoes to weigh somewhere between 250 and 400 grams or more for a high-mileage version, depending on terrain type, brand, size, and whether it is for a man or woman. For example, the Salomon XA Pro 3D weighs around 410 grams

for the men's version and 354 grams for the women's version, depending on sizes. Lightweight racing/performance trail shoes are also available, offering the compromise of less protection and durability in exchange for less weight.

Stability versus neutral type – high-mileage running shoes

As discussed above, high-mileage running shoes have cushioning and stability features built into the midsole. Each brand will have it's own spin on how to achieve a similar function. These are targeted towards helping runners to prevent injuries by dampening the impact forces and reducing the amount of over-pronation, which are commonly identified contributing factors to running-related injuries despite the continued lack of strong evidence in current research.[77]

High-mileage running shoes can be further divided into two main functional sub-types. Please note that there are variations in categories and terminology used by other podiatrists and running shoe suppliers. I use the following system because I feel it best communicates the different shoe types and their features when referring to running-shoe stores.

1. Stability running shoes
   a) Mild stability – for mild to moderate over-pronation
   b) Moderate stability – for moderate to severe over-pronation
   c) Maximum stability – for severe over-pronation

2. Neutral running shoes
   a) Firm (torsion/bend) neutral – for a neutral foot function type
   b) Soft (torsion/bend) neutral – for under-pronation (runner with a typically rigid high-arched foot type)

1. Stability running shoes

The reason for increased stability features is that over-pronation, as mentioned earlier, has long been considered a risk factor for running-related injuries, despite the lack of strong evidence in the research.[78]

This type of running shoe is traditionally designed for runners whose feet over-pronate anywhere from mildly to severely, and typically for runners who heel and midfoot strike. Basically, the more your feet over-pronate, the greater the amount of stability that is required in the running shoe. Typical stability features include a stiff shank to increase torsional stiffness and higher-density foam through the medial side of the midsole (medial posting). Because the firmer foam is placed on the medial side of the shoe – from the heel to the end of the arch area, although there are a few exceptions that go past this point – it only provides a potential benefit if these parts of the foot contact in a heel-to-toe fashion. So, forefoot striking negates the ability of this shoe to provide possible over-pronation support.

The term 'dual-density midsole' is still commonly used to describe this feature. Midsole functional designs have become a little more complex in recent years, offering what is called 'dynamic support', the aim of which is to guide the foot through the stance phase of gait as opposed to trying to block or control motion.

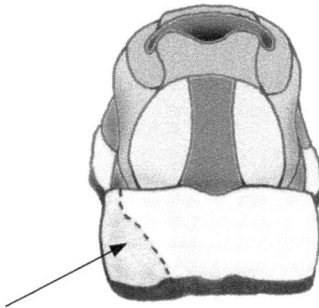

Medially posted, dual density feature
of a right traditional stability shoe

How much stability shoes can actually reduce the amount of over-pronation and do what the brands claim they do is arguable. One particular study, where the researchers used bone pins to determine what effect different footwear construction had on altering the path of movement of the skeleton and lower extremities, found that 'changes were small and not systematic'.[79] That is, not every runner responded the same way to the stability features.

Significantly, the authors (Nigg, Baltich, Hoerzer & Enders 2015) proposed a new paradigm that could possibly replace previously potentially inappropriate paradigms in relation to cushioning and trying to reduce over-pronation to prevent injuries. They called it the 'preferred movement path' paradigm:

> [T]he skeleton of an individual athlete attempts for a given task (e.g., heel–toe running) to stay in the same movement path, 'the preferred movement path'.[80]

Further as muscle activity is used to ensure the skeleton stays in this preferred path, they also proposed a change to the definition of a 'good' running shoe to one that allows less muscle activity compared to a 'bad' running shoe to ensure the skeleton moves in the preferred path. [81]

This challenges the traditional method of prescribing running shoes that has been used for decades and is based purely on the assumption that stability running shoes will reduce the amount of pronation and therefore help to prevent running injuries.

2. Neutral running shoes

A neutral running shoe can be simply described as having the same density foam throughout the whole midsole (i.e., no dual-density feature). The main injury prevention role of this shoe involves dampening impact forces without interfering with the natural pronation of the foot. This type of running shoe is also traditionally prescribed for a variety of foot function types, from those whose feet have an adequate amount of pronation to feet that are rigid and over-supinate.

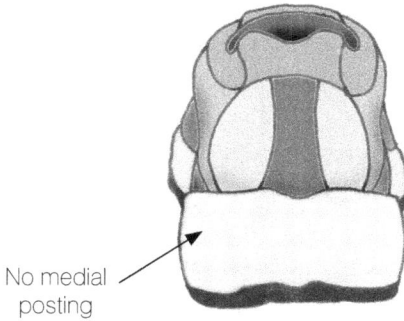

No medial posting

Neutral running shoe (no medial posting) – right shoe

As described in chapter 3, when the foot re-supinates during late midstance to toe-off, all of the bones move into a more stable position, more closely packed together, to allow more efficient transfer of forces to the ground. If the foot over-supinates and rolls out too far during midstance, there are no running shoes that attempt to reduce this movement. The main reason for this is that an over-supinating foot is typically a rigid, high-arched foot type, and placing harder foam in the lateral part of the midsole where runners typically strike (heel inverted position), would potentially compound the problem of this foot type being a poor shock absorber.

One intervention that can help a runner whose feet over-supinate, and who suffers from a running injury related to this movement, involves incorporating lateral wedge padding (valgus padding) underneath the insole of the running shoes to counteract the foot rolling out. A podiatrist can build this modification into the appropriate foot orthosis device if it proves helpful and is required in the longer term.

a) **Firm neutral** – This shoe has stiffness built into the midsection of the midsole (looking at the shoe lengthwise) usually in the form of the plastic shank that has already been described. This provides resistance to torsion and bending. This feature aims to reduce the stresses on the joints of the midfoot and the soft tissue structures of the medial longitudinal arch. The midsole only bends at the forefoot where the metatarsal phalangeal joints of the feet bend. Bending in this area still allows for the windlass mechanism (chapter 3) to work. There is usually a certain amount of resistance to this bend to reduce the forces through the forefoot during propulsion. This form of neutral shoe is traditionally recommended if a runner's foot has a moderate to hypermobile range of movement but maintains overall efficient foot function during running gait.

b) **Soft neutral** – These running shoes allow more flex versus the firm neutral shoe. Instead of bending at the location of the metatarsal phalangeal joints, they often bend through the middle of the midsole (when holding the shoe in your hands to conduct the test). Further, twisting the shoe reveals less torsional resistance as well. Allowing for more flex means that the shoe is designed not to interfere with the wearers foot function. A rigid high-arch foot type that potentially does not allow enough pronation, may be one example of where this shoe is recommended.

7

Non-traditional running shoes

One can speculate that the reason non-traditional running shoe designs enter the mainstream market relatively successfully is because, as mentioned in chapter 5, despite advances in traditional running shoe design, there has been no decrease in the rate of running injuries since the 1970s.[82]

Potential shoe-related reasons that have been suggested for no change in the rate of running-related injuries include traditional running shoes with higher-heeled cushioned midsoles which, although comfortable, may actually limit proprioception and make it easier for runners to strike on their heels with higher impact. Further, many traditional running shoes have arch supports and stiffened soles which, it has been suggested, may lead to weaker foot muscles and reduced strength in the arches.[83] These suggestions have received increasing media attention in recent years, particularly in the late 2000s, despite having relied heavily on anecdotal evidence (i.e., personal accounts) rather than scientific evidence.

For example, consider the popular running book that was published in 2009, *Born to Run: A hidden tribe, superathletes, and the greatest race the world has never seen*. The author claimed that the famed Tarahumara ultra-runners from northern Mexico were phenomenal endurance runners in part because they ran only in minimal sandals. They also apparently did not suffer from modern-day running injuries. Traditional or modern-day running shoes were suggested to be the cause of many contemporary running injuries.[84] After *Born to Run* was launched, with its claims of minimal injuries and 'superathletes', it is clear with the help of the media how barefoot and minimalist running instantly became more popular. This was despite there being no scientific support for the claims.

Interestingly, one positive result that emerged was the generation of more interest in the scientific community in relation to minimalist running and its potential benefits in terms of reducing the incidence of running injuries while also potentially improving performance.[85] The idea that you can decrease injury risk and improve performance by changing from a traditional running shoe to a minimalist running shoe is still one of the most popular topics in the running world. (The potential benefits of minimalist running are discussed shortly.)

Running shoe brands are obviously aware that runners are being exposed to all this information and that people are exploring non-traditional options. As a result, more models within traditional brands are being designed with non-traditional features, including minimal cushioning, maximum cushioning, lower heel pitches, no heel counters, more flexible (twist and bend) midsoles, and rocker soles that are very stiff, to name a few. Nevertheless, most traditional brands at present still prioritise catering for the mainstream running community, with traditional running shoe design making up the bulk of sales.

Non-traditional running shoes fall into two main categories:

1. minimalist running shoes
2. maximalist running shoes

Minimalist running shoes

Minimalist running shoes provide minimal interference with the natural movement of the foot and are typically characterised by low weight, high flexibility, low cushioning, low heel to toe drop, and low stack height.[86] The heel drop between different minimalist running shoes can vary between 0 and 8-mm (compared to the 10–12 mm typically seen in traditional running shoes).[87] Most are void of motion control features, and at their most minimal, often provide just a thin layer of outsole to protect the skin from rough surfaces and sharp objects.

Minimalist zero-drop running shoe

There is definitely a spectrum of minimalist running shoes and some confusion about how minimalist a running shoe may actually be. For example, many minimalist-classed shoes are still quite cushioned, with a moderate amount of stack height. What may define them within this category is the lower than traditional heel-drop height, high flexibility, and lightness. For example, the Saucony Kinvara 10 has a stack height of 23-mm at the heel and 19-mm at the forefoot. Although there is still plenty of foam under the foot, it is considered a minimalist running shoe because it has a 4-mm heel drop, as well as being flexible and light.

The variety of minimalist running shoes definitely offers a few positives, despite confusion amongst some consumers. One potential benefit is that we can use 'in-between' running shoes that attempt to garner benefits from both categories (i.e., traditional and minimalist) without having to go suddenly from one extreme to the other. Another potential benefit is that the variety of minimalist shoes means you can more slowly transition from traditional running shoes into the minimalism category depending how closely you want to get to barefoot running.

Note: if you are considering this, I would highly recommend consulting a suitably experienced podiatrist to help you transition and work with you to formulate an overall transitional plan. This transition may include referral to a physiotherapist as well as an alteration in your current running program, to allow soft tissue structures to adapt to the changes of load in the body that occur when using minimalist running shoes.

In general, minimalist running shoes are designed and used with the premise of providing the same purported injury prevention benefits of running barefoot, in particular, changing a runner's gait to strike more anteriorly on the foot, as well as running with a shorter stride length and a higher step rate.[88]

When running barefoot on hard surfaces, such as bitumen, it is uncomfortable to land heavily on your heels and so, supposedly, it naturally encourages us to land on the forefoot.[89] This has the effect of dampening impact forces, in part due to the ankle bending during impact but also the Achilles tendon and calf muscles eccentrically (lengthening movement of muscle) loading on foot strike.[90] The plantar fascia is also thought to play an important shock-absorbing role.[91] As explained in chapter 4, striking on the forefoot, when compared to heel striking, has been shown to significantly decrease the impact transient (burst of energy or force) on foot strike, which may be potentially beneficial in the prevention of running injuries.[92] In particular, a high-impact transient has been associated with tibial stress fractures and plantar fasciitis.[93]

It is important, however, to understand that changes to a runner's gait may not occur automatically while running in minimalist shoes. Because there is still something on the feet, it is not a true representation of the barefoot condition. Ankle and knee mechanics while running barefoot have been shown to be different to all shoe conditions, including minimalist running shoes, indicating that minimalist running shoes cannot entirely replicate the mechanics of running barefoot.[94] Moreover, it has been suggested that without the sensory feedback between the soles of the feet and the surface of the ground, a minimalist runner may not have the complete neural cueing to convert to a forefoot strike pattern.[95] Even a thin rubber outsole may impede the body's ability to convert from heel striking.

Despite not being able to completely replicate all the benefits of barefoot running, other benefits of minimalist shoes have been identified. One such benefit related to injury prevention may be improved intrinsic foot muscle strength. For example, one study found that various intrinsic muscles in the foot became larger after a 12-week minimalist running training regime: '[E]ndurance running in minimal support footwear with a 4-mm offset or less makes greater use of the spring like function of the longitudinal arch, thus leading to greater demands on the intrinsic muscles that support the arch, thereby strengthening the foot.'[96]

Minimalist shoes have also been connected to improved running performance in terms of helping to improve running economy. Oxygen consumption, or VO2, is the most common way to measure how much work is being done by the body while running. Improving running economy means that less oxygen is consumed if all other variables stay the same for a certain running distance. One study found that across a range of running speeds, VO2 increased by approximately one per cent for each 100 grams of mass added to each shoe.[97] Another study found that VO2 was significantly lower with minimalist running shoes in comparison to traditional running shoes, and much closer to that identified with barefoot running.[98] This is supported by a meta-analysis, a type of review that uses a statistical approach to combine the results from multiple studies in an effort to increase power, improve estimates of the size of the effect, and/or resolve uncertainty when reports disagree, by Cheung & Ngai (2016) who concluded that 'running in lighter shoes may require less oxygen consumption and theoretically the lower oxygen cost may improve long distance running performance'.[99]

Another potential benefit of minimalist running shoes is that if they do truly promote a forefoot strike, as barefoot running does, they are tapping into the body's natural springs (mainly via the Achilles tendon and the ligaments under the arch of the foot). When these structures are lengthened during a forefoot strike, they store elastic energy that returns during the propulsion phase of running gait (see chapter 4).

Potential injury risks of minimalist running shoes

Despite the potential injury prevention and performance benefits of running in minimalist running shoes, potential running injury risks have been identified. For example, striking on the forefoot places greater load and demand on the Achilles tendon and the metatarsal bones of the foot.[100] Without adequate time and training to adapt to this increase in load, injury to these structures may occur.[101]

This potential for injury risk is further supported by a high-quality random controlled trial (the gold standard for ascertaining the efficacy and safety of a treatment). Fuller, Thewlis, Buckley, Brown, Hamill & Tsiros (2017) compared running-related pain and injury between minimalist and traditional running shoes in trained runners as well as the interactions between shoe type, body mass, and weekly training distance. They found that 'greater pain was experienced with minimalist shoes especially when training distance exceeded more than 35km/week' and 'more runners sustained an injury compared to conventional (traditional) shoes as well as the risk of sustaining an injury increased as your body mass increased above 71.4kg'. They concluded that 'runners should limit weekly training distance in minimalist shoes to avoid running-related pain... Also, heavier runners are at a greater risk of injury when running in minimalist shoes.'[102]

The take-home message, and my advice, is that if you are considering incorporating minimalist running, make sure you seek face-to-face advice from a suitably experienced podiatrist and/or other health professional who can review such risks with you and guide you on how best to proceed. This is especially true for beginner and novice runners. In particular, it has been suggested that some running injuries may be caused by transitioning too quickly from traditional to minimalist running shoes.[103]

Maximalist running shoes

This is a running shoe with a large amount of midsole stack height. Such running shoes commonly have what is called a rocker or meta-rocker bottom design built in. This is because the thick forefoot stack height inherently creates a stiffer forefoot section, and without the rocker design, the transition from heel to forefoot would not be as smooth or efficient.

Large stack height

Maximalist running shoe

The Hoka One One Bondi 6 is an example of a maximalist shoe. This model has a 36-mm midsole thickness at the heel and a 32-mm thickness at the forefoot. This can be compared to a more traditional running shoe design like the Asics Kayano 26 men's version, which has a 29-mm thickness at the heel and a 19-mm thickness at the forefoot.

Interestingly, despite the larger stack height at both heel and forefoot, there is only a 4-mm heel drop in the Hoka One One Bondi 6 when compared to a 10-mm heel drop in the traditional designed Asics Kayano 26 example. The lower heel drop makes this running shoe potentially conform more closely to the premise of a minimalist running shoe, especially in comparison to its higher-pitched traditional running shoe counterpart.

The potential benefits of the lower heel drop have already been discussed. The maximal cushioning in this shoe can be seen as an attempt to more closely mimic running on cushioned terrain as our bodies were better designed to do, something that is covered in more detail shortly, as well as whether this maximum cushioning actually provides benefits in reducing impact forces.

The maximalist nature of these shoes often gives the impression that they are going to be heavier than traditional running shoes. This is not the case, as they are deceptively lighter than many traditional high-mileage running shoes, despite their often heavier, 'brick-like' appearance. For example, let's compare the stability versions in size 9 men's in a Hoka One One and a couple of traditional brand models. The Hoka Arahi 3 weighs in at around 272 grams in comparison to the Asics Kayano 26, which weighs in at around 315 grams. The Brooks Adrenaline 20 is about 302 grams, whereas the New Balance 1260 v6 is around 326 grams. This reduction in weight can potentially improve running economy, as discussed previously.

I have used a few examples of the Hoka One One brand mainly because it is widely known, as well as having been a trailblazer in this category. To briefly explain the origins, the meta-rocker design (which involved increasing the stack height) of the Hoka One One shoes was originally built into the shoes at a time when the two ultra-running co-founders of the company were trying to improve downhill running. Their aim was to keep a runner's momentum going, like a wheel on a bike, as opposed to a series of stops and starts.[104] This goes against the traditional running shoe design that allows for bending, in particular where the metatarsal phalangeal joints (ball of the foot) bend. It also challenges what we understand about the biomechanics of feet, which usually require efficient bending of the toes and consequent activation of the windlass mechanism (chapter 3) to allow the foot to re-supinate (roll out) in time for efficient propulsion.

There is no doubt that maximalist shoes have become more popular over the years. For example, in 2017, for the first time, and then again in 2018, Hoka One One was the most popular running shoe at the Kona Ironman Triathlon in Hawaii, one of the most famous – as well as one of the hardest to qualify for – ironman triathlons in the world.[105] It seems, that as a result of this increasing popularity, more research has been done on the potential benefits and risks.

Specifically, the maximum cushioning that these shoes provide has been of particular interest to researchers. It seems natural to assume that the more cushioning you provide underfoot, the better the dampening of impact forces must be. Therefore, the maximalist shoe must do the best job of this. However, in one study, researchers found that running in highly cushioned maximalist shoes increased rather than dampened impact loading, especially at faster running speeds.[106] Similar results were found by other scholars whose findings suggest that maximalist shoes may not dampen impact forces during level and downhill treadmill running.[107]

However, the reason that maximalist running shoes may not provide the dampening of impact forces they were designed to produce remains poorly understood. One possible explanation, according to Kulmala, Kosonen, Nurminen & Avela (2018), is that maximum cushioned running shoes most likely affect the spring-like running mechanics (provided in part by the Achilles tendon and plantar foot ligaments) when compared to traditional running shoes. Notably, they add that when wearing maximum cushioned running shoes, the runner's legs became stiffer due to lower compression compared to runners wearing traditional running shoes. Stiffer legs were suggested to have the effect of decelerating the body's entire mass and therefore negating the benefit of the extra cushioning.[108]

The longitudinal stiffness that exists in maximalist shoes is also a common treatment used by podiatrists for forefoot conditions such as osteoarthritis, metatarsalgia, and metatarsal stress fractures. Injured joints in the forefoot in particular can benefit from the stiffness. Less bending means less force is applied to the damaged joint structures.

The plantar pressure of the forefoot during the *propulsion* phase of running is similarly reduced with a rocker, which is also helpful for patients suffering from metatarsalgia or a history of stress fractures. A rocker-bottom shoe may thus be helpful in helping prevent both of these injuries from occurring in the first place, particularly during endurance running.[109]

An even more interesting potential use of the rocker or meta-rocker design is for patients suffering from Achilles tendinopathy, one of the most common running-related injuries.[110] One study found that rocker shoes reduced Achilles tendon loading in both running and walking, making it a potential useful adjunct to treating patients with chronic Achilles tendinopathy.[111] However, a further study by the same authors indicated that rocker shoes significantly increased work at the knees. So, despite the potential to decrease the mechanical load on the Achilles tendon, rocker shoes could increase the risk of overuse injuries of the knee joint.[112]

As a runner, such information may be important to consider, as it may impact on whether you choose to use a particular running shoe as your only running shoe or as part of a rotation. For example, a maximalist shoe with a rocker-bottom design may be useful in your running shoe rotation if you have a long-standing history of Achilles tendon problems or forefoot conditions. Alternatively, you may choose not to include this type of shoe in your rotation, or at least use it less frequently, if you have a chronic knee condition.

As always, it is best to seek professional guidance from a suitably experienced podiatrist before potentially looking at changing running shoes solely to help with running injuries. As explained in section 3, they should definitely not be used in isolation to treat an injury, but may be a useful adjunct to an overall treatment plan.

FAQ #6: Which is the best category of running shoes (traditional, minimalist, or maximalist) for preventing running injuries?

Unfortunately, there does not seem to be one category of running shoe that is better than the others to help prevent injuries. For example, traditional running shoes do not seem to have made a difference at all in terms of injury prevention. Despite all of the advancements and money spent on traditional running shoe technology, there has been no decrease in the frequency of running injuries since the 1970s.[113] There is also a lack of evidence to suggest that changing to a minimalist running shoe will be any more protective against injury. The same may be said for maximalist shoes, as there is a significant lack of high-quality studies to suggest otherwise.[114]

It is important to remember that not all of the blame for injuries can be laid on running shoes. Most running injuries are multifactorial, and yet advances in other areas of running and exercise science also seem to have failed to lower overall running injury risk.

Other reasons for this lack of advancement may be related to changes in the running population since the 1970s, that is changes in the demographics. According to Nigg, Baltich, Hoerzer & Enders (2015), runners in the 1970s and 1980s were different to runners in the 2000s in that they were primarily male (75%), more dedicated, aiming to win, skinny, and primarily ran. Today's runners are made up of slightly more females (54%). Also, they are mainly 'recreational runners who run a marathon to finish, some are overweight and most are involved in cross-training activities … Furthermore, the populations studied in various epidemiological studies were not the same. Some authors studied new runners while others studied competitive runners.'[115]

Others have suggested that variations in definitions of what constitutes a running injury may contribute to the problem of researchers not being able to compare injury frequencies accurately.[116] Hence, 'there is a need for future researchers to standardise the definition of a running injury so this does not become a continual confounding variable.'[117]

Interestingly, off the back of their research, Nigg, Baltich, Hoerzer & Enders (2015) suggested a new paradigm, the 'comfort filter' paradigm, to help explain why there has been no change in the risk of running injuries over time. I find this an important consideration for runners trying to decide which running shoes to purchase.

The results from their study suggest that different runners need different features in a running shoe to feel comfortable (e.g., stability versus no stability) and that 'this is associated with a lower movement-related injury frequency than shoe conditions that are less comfortable' and 'running shoe conditions that are comfortable are associated with less oxygen consumption than conditions that are less comfortable'.[118] The last point is a significant consideration when choosing running shoes for performance. The 'comfort filter' paradigm they suggested states that, 'when selecting a running shoe an athlete selects a comfortable product using his/her own comfort filter ... This automatically reduces the injury risk and may be a possible explanation for the fact that there does not seem to have been a trend in running injury frequency over time'.[119]

FAQ #7: Which is the best category of running shoes (traditional, minimalist, or maximalist) for performance?

One thing we do know is that lightness is a very important factor. For every 100 grams added to each pair of running shoes, running economy decreases by one per cent.[120] However, this factor needs to be carefully considered in conjunction with a runner's experience and conditioning, because the lighter the shoe gets, the less supportive and protective it is. For some beginner and novice recreational runners, even participating in short-distance fun runs in shoes that are too light or minimalist could be injurious. For example, as weight goes down, there can be a corresponding lower heel drop. For heel strikers, this may increase the impact forces created by less cushioning. A lower heel drop also means more load is placed on the Achilles tendon.

There is no definitive answer to the question of which actual category of running shoe is better for performance, as there is conflicting evidence in the research. While some additional running shoe features are very important, minimalist running shoes on the more minimal end of the scale obviously have a clear advantage when it comes to lower weight. In addition, as already mentioned, Nigg et al. (2015) have suggested as part of their 'comfort filter' paradigm that running conditions that are more comfortable are associated with less oxygen consumption and better performance.[121]

Perl, Daoud & Lieberman (2012) concluded in their study that:

[R]unners wearing minimalist running shoes are modestly but significantly more economical than traditionally shod runners, regardless of strike type, after controlling for shoe mass and stride frequency. The likely cause of this difference is more elastic energy storage and release in the lower extremity during minimal-shoe running.[122]

Fuller, Thewlis, Tsiros, Brown & Buckley (2016) concluded in their study 'that running in minimalist shoes acutely improves time trial performance and running economy'. Further, being lighter in weight improved running economy, but did not improve time trial performance. Faster running speeds were also suggested to help running economy the most. Running in minimalist running shoes perceived to be more comfortable than traditional running shoes was also related to improvement in running performance over five kilometres.[123]

Conversely, it must be noted that cushioning in running shoes has been suggested to help reduce the muscular effort needed to cushion impact with the ground, thereby reducing metabolic cost and improving running economy.[124] Tung, Franz & Kram (2014) concluded that 'the design of road racing shoes on paved surfaces should not overemphasize weight minimalization at the expense of cushioning'.[125] Further, Worobets, Wannop, Tomaras & Stefanyshyn (2014) showed that '[r]unning with softer and more resilient midsoles were found to influence running economy by 1% on average during treadmill and over-ground experiments'.[126]

It appears that a number of running shoe design variables can influence running economy and performance. This is further backed up by a systematic review by Fuller, Bellenger, Thewlis, Tsiros & Buckley (2015) that looked at the effect of footwear on running performance and running economy in distance runners. Key points from this review include that running shoes with greater shoe cushioning, stiffness (longitudinal stiffness), and comfort were associated with improved running economy.[127] Further, running in light shoes or barefoot reduced metabolic cost when compared with running in heavy shoes, but there was no difference in metabolic cost between running in light shoes and running barefoot.[128]

An ideal running shoe for performance would thereby feature a combination of all of these elements: lightweight, yet cushioned and longitudinally stiff. With this in mind, it is time to look more closely at the controversial Nike Vaporfly and Alphafly series, which incorporate all of these important features, including innovative design and technology.

Nike Vaporfly and Alphafly series – the shoes that seemingly changed running forever

The 4% tag on the original Nike Vaporfly model (Nike Vaporfly 4% – weighing in at a relatively light 196 grams for men's size US 9) came from a 2017 study published in the journal *Sports Medicine*, funded by Nike, and conducted in the University of Boulder's Locomotion Lab. This study showed that, on average, amongst the 18 runners tested, the energetic cost of running when wearing these shoes was lowered by 4%. With this improvement in running economy, the researchers predicted that top athletes wearing these shoes could run substantially faster and achieve the first sub-2-hour marathon.[129] Further independent studies demonstrated similar results.[130]

One feature reported to help improve running economy is the midsole material. As mentioned previously, each brand has their own proprietary blend of midsole material designed to improve performance, amongst other things. For example, in the Nike ZoomX Vaporfly Next% model (187 grams for men's size US 9) the properties of the midsole material, a version of Pebax foam that Nike calls ZoomX, is reported to return 87% of energy when compared to two previous high-performance Nike running shoes that returned 75.9% and 65.5%, respectively.[131] Interestingly, this particular Vaporfly shoe version also has an 8-mm heel to toe drop (down from an 11-mm heel drop in the previous VaporFly 4%), which is at the higher end of the definition of a minimalist shoe. This shoe could also be defined as a maximalist running shoe with its very large stack height when compared to traditional running shoes. The height at the heel of the Nike ZoomX Vaporfly Next% model is up to 40-mm, depending on the shoe size. In particular, the large stack height allows enough room to accommodate its most controversial feature, the curved, spoon-shaped carbon fibre plate.

Nike were not the first to introduce carbon fibre plates into running shoes, but they are the only ones that appear to have successfully harnessed their mechanical advantage. Most people believe that the mechanical advantage of the carbon plate built into the shoe provides a snap-back effect that boosts energy return during the propulsion phase of running gait. However, it is in fact the stiffness created by the carbon fibre plate in conjunction with the appropriately placed spoon-shaped curve that really improves the energetic cost of running by positively changing the mechanical leverage of the ankle joint and the foot–toe joints (metatarsal phalangeal joints).[132] Basically, the calf muscles, Achilles tendon, plantar ligaments, and other muscles of the feet do not have to work as hard on every stride and do not fatigue as quickly through the course of a race. This means that all things being equal, you can run faster, for longer.

The placement of the carbon fibre plate also provides structure for the very large stack height of the lightweight, energy-returning ZoomX midsole material. Without it, such a large amount of this particular foam might be too unstable. How these elements work together is part of Nike's design genius and allows this shoe to provide significant performance gains.

This performance improvement in some runners underpins the major controversy surrounding the use of these shoes, particularly whether they create an unfair disadvantage for runners unable to wear these shoes in competition. For example, some elite marathon runners have improved their times by up to three to four minutes wearing these shoes.

In January 2020, World Athletics announced they were going to rule on whether these running shoes would be allowed in official competition. This was after Kenya's Eliud Kipchoge broke the two-hour mark in October 2019 (in a non-competition, heavily runner- and car-wind-assisted and choreographed course) wearing, at the time an unnamed and unreleased model. The next day, Kenya's Brigid Kosgei smashed the women's marathon world record (that was set in 2003) by 81 seconds at the Chicago Marathon wearing the Nike ZoomX Vaporfly NEXT% model.

World Athletics announced in early February 2020 that the design of the Nike ZoomX Vaporfly NEXT% and soon to be named Nike Air Zoom Alphafly NEXT% models would be considered legal and allowed in competition. New rules were also announced at the same time governing the thickness of the midsole stack height (maximum of 40-mm) and only permitting one level of carbon fibre plating. In addition, shoe manufacturers were prohibited from allowing athletes to run in prototypes, meaning that their competition shoes must be available to the general public for a period of four months prior to use in competition.

Interestingly, it was rumoured that Nike's Air Zoom Alphafly NEXT% prototype, which Eliud Kipchoge had worn when he broke two hours, had an even larger stack height (reportedly 51-mm at the heel), three carbon fibre plates to provide structure for the large amount of ZoomX foam, and two additional pressurised air cushions built between the plates to further aide propulsion. This rumour was later refuted by Nike.

The latest iteration retail release version of the Nike Air Zoom Alphafly NEXT% sits within the design ruling guidelines. Although it is said that Nike reduced the stack height from the original prototype and the shoe now only has one carbon fibre plate, it still has the two pressurised air cushions (air pods) at the front. Nike claims these air pods return up to 90% of absorbed energy; even more than the ZoomX foam which, as already mentioned, reportedly returns up to 87% of absorbed energy. At the time of writing, the exact mechanisms of these pressurised air pods are unknown, but they are another attempt to refine performance-enhancing technology.

The ruling by World Athletics has been met with some criticism, especially as many feel the integrity of the sport has been and continues to be compromised. For example, there is an uneven playing field for elite runners who are not sponsored by Nike. There is also the junior athlete whose family may not be able to afford the new technology, placing them at a competitive disadvantage. It has even been suggested that some competitive runners are unable to advance their athletic careers because they are not wearing these shoes.

Running is now no longer just about human conditioning; it is also about how technology can help to improve running performance. Long distance running had previously been viewed as a 'pure' sport, but this has obviously changed. It will be interesting to see how the future plays out in this arena, particularly the effect on the athletes themselves, and whether the sport is viewed more negatively by spectators. It may also have an impact on future running shoe design rulings, especially if further dominance by one particular brand continues.

Nike's role in breaking the two-hour marathon

Breaking the two-hour marathon mark was once thought impossible. Although elite marathon times have come down over recent years, especially since Nike's development of the Vaporfly in 2016, it was suggested that to run it under two hours would require almost perfect race day conditions as well as the right runners at their peaks, pushing and helping each other.

No doubt it was this intrigue, as well as the commercial motivation of potentially being the first to do it, that drove Nike to initially invest in this endeavour and continue to innovate.

If you are unaware, the Nike-sponsored world record holder, Eliud Kipchoge, failed in his first attempt (2 hours and 25 seconds in Monza, Italy, May 2017) but succeeded in his second attempt (1 hour, 59 minutes and 40 seconds in Vienna, Austria, October 2019). To emphasise this extraordinary accomplishment, consider that Kipchoge was running approximately 17 seconds per 100 metres, 1 minute 8 seconds per 400 metres and 2 minutes 50 seconds per kilometre for 42.195 km. If you have not viewed a replay of the event, I would highly recommend it.

Now, this feat did not qualify as an official world record (at the time of writing, the world record is 2 hours, 1 minute, and 39 seconds, held by the same runner, Eliud Kipchoge) because of the optimal running conditions and assistance provided. In particular, Kipchoge had a rotating pacing team of 41 runners working in shifts to maintain a seven-man, reverse V-shaped formation to protect him from wind drag. There was also a pacing car out front providing head wind protection. In normal race conditions, runners can often be solo, or at times leading a pack, with no protection from the wind. Of all the factors leading to the breaking of the two-hour mark, it has been suggested this was the most significant. Nike's shoes had already demonstrated their worth in bringing official competition times closer to the mark over the four years in which they had been in production.

So, it does seem that a running shoe can help with performance. It also could be seen as having borrowed features from all of the different shoe categories – lightweight, yet cushioned and longitudinally stiff. And, at least for the time being, one brand appears to stand out. However other brands have followed suit with similar carbon fibre, maximum stacked shoes already available on the market, all initially in readiness for the now postponed Tokyo 2020 Olympics.

Yet, it must be noted that not all runners who choose these racing or performance shoes enjoy the same reported performance gains. There are also potentially unexplored injury risks associated with changing the mechanics of the body and wearing these shoes too often. For the average recreational runner looking to improve running performance, there remain definitely more important factors to consider prior to your next event before purchasing a very expensive pair of performance-enhancing running shoes. An in-depth description of these are outside the scope of this book, but they include factors such as efficient running technique, running programming, strength training, and nutrition. Seeking face-to-face guidance with an experienced running coach is a great place to start to address these areas.

FAQ #8: Which is the best running shoe brand?

Even though Nike may have a performance edge for the time being, the short, overall answer to this broad question is that there isn't one best running shoe brand. Some have models that are more comfortable, supportive and react better underfoot for some runners while other brands will better suit others. These factors may even change from season to season, as brands sometimes change the build and design features of their models.

This question is different to 'What is the most popular running shoe brand?' This is because what is most popular isn't necessarily what is best for *you*. It is easy to get caught up in popular trends and potentially be swayed by marketing.

In terms of quality, brands spend millions of dollars every year on research and development, continually seeking ways to refine their technology to improve injury prevention and establish support, comfort, and performance edges over their rivals.

Section 3 | Running foot tips

Running injuries are often multifactorial, making it important to address a number of factors to reduce the high risk of injury. Remember, your feet and running shoes are only a part of the bigger picture and should not be the whole focus. Setting realistic goals, planning your running week (e.g., how often to run without overdoing it), and running with correct technique are also important. Keeping your cadence in check to prevent overstriding and excessive vertical displacement, incorporating whole body strength, adding flexibility and core strength into your week, and scheduling adequate rest days are also key. So too are building variation within your running sessions, incorporating cross training into your running cycles, and making sure your nutrition and hydration are adequate, especially to aid recovery between running sessions.

While all are important, these factors fall outside the scope of this book, and there exists a plethora of great books on these topics. The best option I recommend is to seek face-to-face advice from the right person who can help you with these factors and, more importantly, cater for your individual needs.

For example, I advise my running patients to visit a running-experienced physiotherapist for a full screening to identify individual weaknesses and to instigate appropriate interventions to address them. Education around running technique drills, ideal cadence, managing load, how often to incorporate your strength exercises, and creating an appropriate program (including rest days) are typically discussed in a consultation – if not already reviewed in my assessment.

I recommend joining a running club, squad, or group with a suitably qualified and experienced running coach who can guide you through your running goals. If you are time poor, there are reputable online coaches available who can guide you via email and/or phone. A suitably qualified running coach can establish an individual program and adjust it accordingly for obstacles such as any running injuries that may occur. Joining a running group – running within a group environment and with other, similarly experienced runners – also helps with motivation.

The following five running foot tips are compiled from some of the most common advice I have given to my running patients over the years, both within the sports podiatry clinic and running shoe store settings.

The aim is to provide you with some useful foot advice to complement the whole running-injury prevention picture. Although there are no magic bullets here, there is some useful advice on running foot health to help you to reduce your running injury risk.

Tip #1

Strengthen your feet

The foot is a common running injury site with a reported 5.7–39.3% incidence rate.[133] Not necessarily related directly to running but in general, foot pain appears sometimes to arise from weakness of the muscles that assist in supporting the medial longitudinal arch of the foot, the intrinsic muscles of the feet. This weakness may lead to excessive strain on other arch-supporting structures, such as the plantar fascia.[134] A recent study found that 'in the current literature there is evidence of a significant association between foot pain and foot muscle weakness when foot pain is of high intensity and primarily measured by toe flexion force'.[135] The study noted, however, that there was inconsistent evidence that lower intensity foot pain is associated with other measures of foot muscle weakness or size. Incorporating strengthening exercises for the intrinsic muscles of the feet is typically recommended when dealing with foot muscle weakness.

Unfortunately for those runners suffering from plantar fasciitis, the most common running condition we tend to see as podiatrists, there is no strong evidence to indicate that increasing foot strength benefits this difficult-to-treat condition.[136] Huffer, Hing, Newton & Clair (2017) in their systematic review, concluded that 'based on the studies reviewed it was not possible to identify the extent to which strengthening interventions that improve foot musculature may benefit symptomatic or at-risk population to plantar fasciitis/ heel pain'.[137]

Not related to any specific injuries but concerning the potential importance of strengthening the intrinsic muscles of the feet, Kelly, Cresswell, Racinais, Whiteley & Lichtwark (2014) showed that 'the activation of the intrinsic foot muscles under load countered the deformation of the arch by increasing the arch stiffness'.[138] This suggests that the stronger the intrinsic foot muscles, the better they may support the arch of runners' feet, making them potentially more resilient to injury. The authors did state however, that 'future studies should examine the influence of the plantar intrinsic foot muscles on longitudinal arch biomechanics during dynamic activities such as walking and running'.[139]

Even though foot strengthening is not the one-stop solution to help prevent all foot injuries, you may benefit from incorporating it into your overall strength routine.

The potential for using barefoot running and minimalist running shoes for foot and lower leg strength

If you are brand new to running, or a recreational runner who has always worn traditional running shoes, incorporating a little bit of barefoot and/or minimalist running could help you increase foot strength, as discussed in chapter 7. According to Miller, Whitcome, Lieberman, Norton & Dyer (2014), various intrinsic muscles in the foot became larger after a 12-week minimalist running training regime. They concluded that 'endurance running in minimal support footwear with 4-mm offset or less makes greater use of the spring-like function of the longitudinal arch, thus leading to greater demands on the intrinsic muscles that support the arch, thereby strengthening the foot'.[140]

It should be noted that a study by Lieberman, Venkadesan, Werbel, Daoud, D'Andrea, Davis, Mang'eni & Pitsiladis (2010) showed that only 50% of heel-striking shoe-wearing runners transitioned automatically to forefoot striking after six weeks of minimalist running training. In the same study they showed that 83% of habitual running shoe wearers still striked on their heel while running barefoot. As a result, they reported that 'impact forces were 8.6% higher and the rate of loading was 700% greater while heel striking barefoot compared to heel striking while wearing shoes'. *Seven hundred per cent!* This has great potential for causing running injuries at least initially while getting used to running barefoot. Further, they suggested that 'reaping the benefits of barefoot running does not occur naturally in everyone; it has to be learnt and in some people they just might not be able to do it'.[141]

If you are considering incorporating barefoot and/or minimalist running, I highly recommend seeking the services of an experienced running practitioner and/or coach who can monitor technique and expertly guide you through a graduated program. Advice from a running-experienced physiotherapist is also critical to make sure your body is in the best physical shape to handle the change. And, depending on your goals, seek advice from a suitably experienced podiatrist in relation to foot strength and how to transition from higher- to lower-drop minimalist shoes before eventually running barefoot.

Even if used as just a small part of your overall program (e.g., warm-up drills), removing your traditional shoes for a little while on soft surfaces, such as grass, may reap you some injury-prevention benefits.

Specific foot-strengthening exercises to do at home

The great thing about most of these exercises is that they do not require expensive equipment or an expensive gym membership. Many can even be done while doing other day-to-day tasks. I have included foot intrinsic and extrinsic muscle exercises to make sure you cover every muscle group related to movement of the foot. Please note that if you experience any pain during these exercises, discontinue them immediately and seek professional advice.

> **Note:** I recommend eventually using weights for the larger extrinsic muscle exercises to place enough force on the feet's tendons, particularly the Achilles tendon to make them as resilient as possible to the repetitive running load you place on

them. Seeking face-to-face advice on how to graduate a weighted loading program and monitor technique is highly recommended once you become proficient with the following simple body weight forms of these exercises.

If you already suffer from a running foot injury, seek professional advice from a suitably experienced podiatrist before attempting these exercises, as there are some conditions in the foot and ankle that may be aggravated further, at least initially, by some of these exercises.

For the purposes of this book, I have broken the following foot-strength exercises into:

1. Small movement
   a) intrinsic muscle exercises
   b) extrinsic muscle exercises
2. Larger movement
   a) extrinsic muscle exercises

1. a) Small movement – intrinsic muscle exercises

Choose two exercises to do each day. They can be performed for one minute each, two to three times per day. Once you get the hang of them, you can do these while sitting, eating, reading, or watching television.

Foot crawls

This exercise helps strengthen the toe plantarflexing (when you point your toes towards the ground), arch-supporting intrinsic muscles under your arch. Sit on a chair near the front and your lower legs perpendicular to the floor, so your heels are directly below your knees. Crawl your feet forward only using your toes, keeping the heels and front of your foot in contact with the ground. When you no longer feel much resistance from the ground under your toes, slide your feet back below your knees, to the starting position, and repeat. You can either work one foot at a time or both. If you find the crawling too easy, place more body weight into your heels. You can even stand up and use your full body weight if you want a challenge once you become stronger.

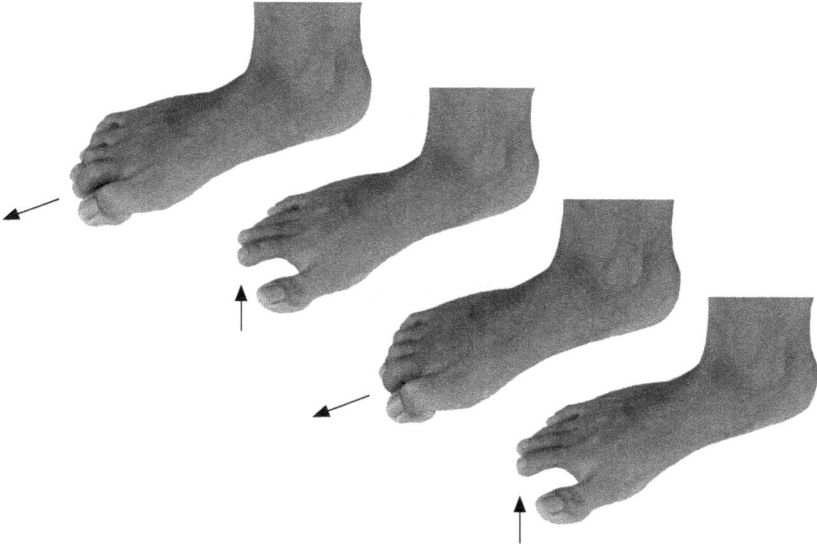

Foot crawls

Toe grabs

Sit on a chair near the front and start with your heels under your knees. Squeeze your toes into the ground, keeping the entire surface of your foot on the ground. Squeeze as hard as you can and hold for 10 seconds, followed by a 10-second rest alternating between wiggling your toes as if playing a piano and spreading your toes apart. These active 10-second rest movements help activate and strengthen the muscles that lie between the metatarsals of your feet.

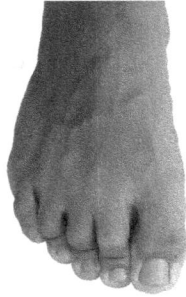

Toe grabs

Toe scrunches with a towel

Spread a bath towel on the floor in front of a chair (ideally on a bare wood or tile surface, so it can slide) so it stretches away from you, with the narrow side facing you. Sit near the front of the seat, your heels under your knees, and your feet on the end of the towel. Using *only* your toes, keeping your feet firmly on the ground, scrunch the towel towards your body. Once you can no longer scrunch the towel effectively, flatten out the towel with your feet and repeat. If you find this exercise easy, place a moderately heavy object (e.g., a textbook) on the far end of the towel to create greater resistance and pull this towards your body.

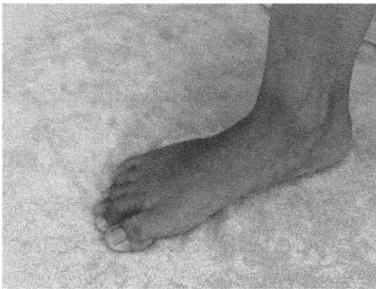

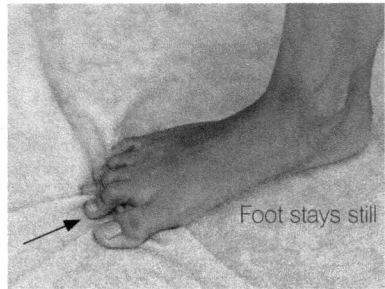

Foot stays still

Towel toe scrunches

Marble, small stone, or Lego pick-ups

Place some marbles, small stones, Lego pieces, or similar objects on the ground. While sitting or standing, use your toes to pick up one object at a time. Grasp the object under your toes by curling them (do not grip it between your toes), lift your foot off the ground, and place the object into an empty container. By standing, you create a single-leg balance exercise, another great balance and foot-strengthening exercise for you described shortly. Once you have filled the container, empty it and repeat until the time is up.

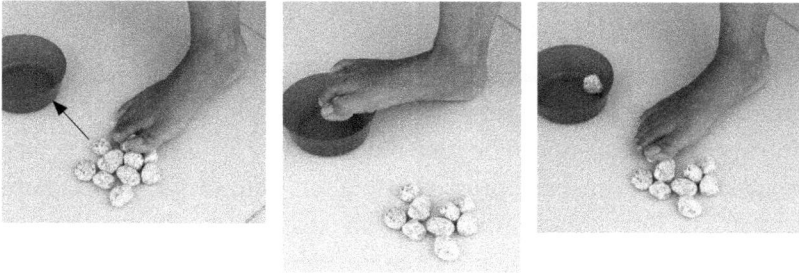

Marble or Lego pick-ups

Big toe taps and lesser toe taps

This is a great exercise that isolates and activates the muscles that plantarflex and dorsiflex the big toes, as well as the muscles that only plantarflex and dorsiflex the lesser (little) toes. You can do each foot individually, or together, while sitting or standing. To start, keep your lesser toes stationary while tapping each big toe on the ground. Then do the reverse: keep your big toe(s) still while tapping your lesser toes on the ground. Alternate every 15 seconds for one minute. Don't be discouraged if you have difficulty at first. Many of my patients initially struggle to isolate their big toes.

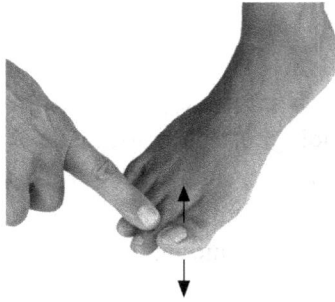

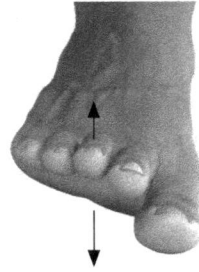

Big toe taps   Lesser tow taps

Big toe downward squeeze

This exercise isolates and strengthens the flexor hallucis brevis muscle, which is an important medial longitudinal arch-supporting intrinsic muscle. You can be seated or standing for this one. Keeping your lesser toes relaxed, press your big toes into the ground as hard as you can. Sometimes I find placing the big toe on a slightly elevated ledge still with the heel on the ground can better activate this muscle. Squeeze and hold for 10 seconds, relax momentarily, and repeat, for approximately one minute.

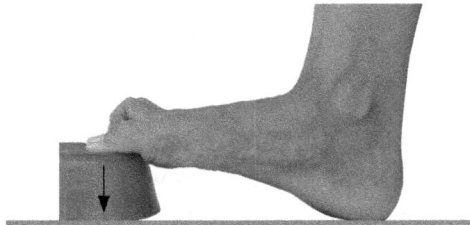

Big toe downward squeeze

Lesser toes downward squeeze

This exercise isolates and strengthens the flexor digitorum brevis muscle which connects to all four lesser toes. It can be done seated or standing. Relax your big toe(s) and squeeze your lesser toes against the ground. Squeeze and hold for 10 seconds, relax momentarily, and repeat, for one minute. If you find this difficult, try elevating your lesser toes slightly on a ledge with the heel still on the ground to better activate this muscle.

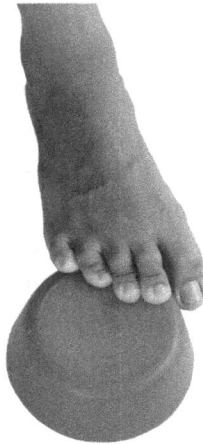

Lesser toes downward squeeze

Lesser toe spreads with big toe squeeze

This exercise strengthens the muscles between the metatarsals of the feet. Lightly squeeze both of your big toes into the ground (or a ledge as demonstrated below) and spread your lesser toes away from your big toes. Move your lesser toes away and back for 20 seconds before resting momentarily. Repeat two more times for just over one minute, to include resting time.

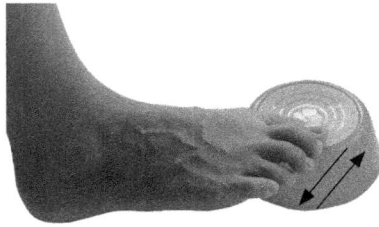

Lesser toe spreads with big toe squeeze

Short foot exercise

This exercise is primarily aimed at strengthening the abductor hallucis brevis muscle which is another important medial longitudinal arch-supporting intrinsic muscle. I find this exercise is best done one foot at a time while seated until it can be done efficiently. Sit on the front edge of a chair with your heel under your knee and keep your full foot on the ground. Slowly shorten the arch of the foot by bringing the ball of the foot towards the heel while paying particular attention not to scrunch your toes. The arch should lift at the same time. Allow your arch to lengthen and lower again and keep repeating the action for a total of one minute.

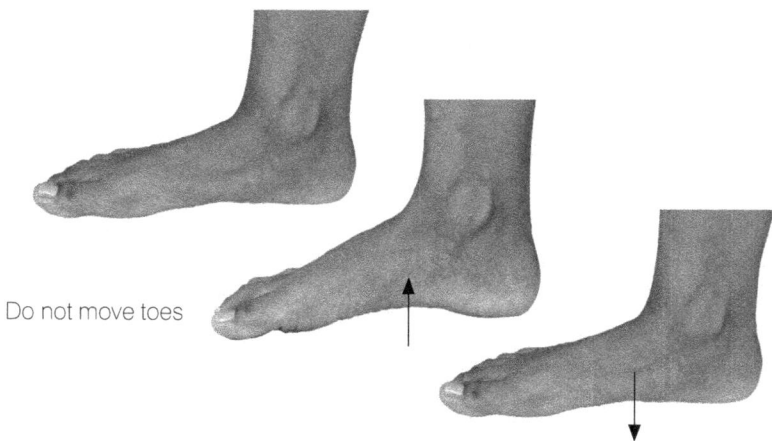

Do not move toes

Short foot exercise

Note: I find the flatter and more flexible a person's foot is, the easier this exercise tends to be. For those with higher arches, you do not need a large lift of the arch for this exercise to be effective. Again, don't be discouraged if you have difficulty at first. Many of my patients initially struggle with this exercise.

1. b) Small movement – extrinsic muscle exercises

For these exercises aim for three times 30 seconds for each leg. Complete 2–3 times per week, with a rest day in between. The exception is the single-leg balance exercise which can be done daily – try it while brushing your teeth.

Isometric ankle inversion exercise

This exercise strengthens the tibialis posterior muscle, whose main roles are foot inversion (turning the feet in) and assisting plantarflexion of the foot. It is also a major supporting structure of the medial longitudinal arch. For this one we are going to work one leg at a time. Start by sitting at the front of a chair parallel to a wall with the closest knee to the wall bent so that your lower leg is tucked under the chair. With your opposing knee bent out at approximately 45 degrees to the ground, place a soccer ball or an object of similar size and firmness between your foot (around the big toe joint area) and the wall. Allowing your foot to point slightly downwards, push the inside of your foot into the ball or object. Push as hard as you can without losing form and hold for 30 seconds. Alternate sides and repeat for the three sets.

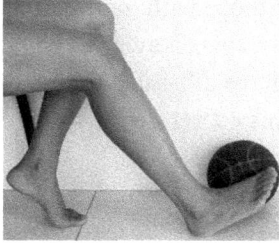

Isometric ankle inversion exercise

Isometric ankle eversion exercise

This exercise helps strengthen the peroneal muscles (peroneus longus and peroneus brevis), the main evertors of your feet (which turn the feet out). They also aid in helping plantarflex the foot (pointing the foot downwards). Sit on a chair parallel to a wall with the right side of your body closest to the wall to start with. Place a soccer ball or similar object between the outside distal half (the half closest to your toes) of your right foot and the wall. With your knees bent out at approximately 45 degrees and your foot pointing slightly downwards, push the ball into the wall as hard as you can. Hold for 30 seconds before swapping sides. Alternate sides and repeat for the three sets.

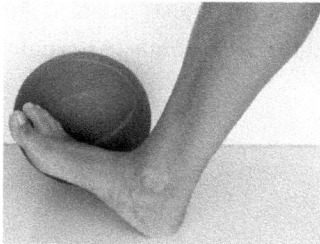

Isometric ankle eversion exercise

Isometric ankle dorsiflexion exercise

This exercise helps strengthen the muscles at the front of your lower leg. These muscles perform the opposite movement to the calf muscles and lift your foot upwards (dorsiflexion). The tibialis anterior muscle which is in this group also assists with foot inversion and supporting the medial longitudinal arch. Sitting on the front edge of a chair, place one foot on top of the other, making sure to cover all the toes. Lift the bottom foot, including the toes, up into the top foot (which provides the resistance) as hard as you can. Hold this position for 30 seconds. Alternate sides and repeat for the three sets.

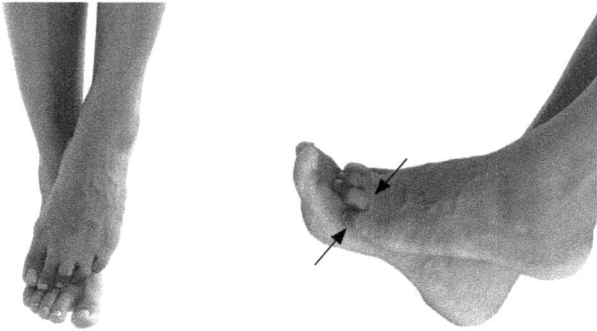

Isometric ankle dorsiflexion exercise

Single leg balance

This is not only a great exercise to improve ankle proprioception and balance but also to strengthen some of the intrinsic and extrinsic muscles of the feet. You will notice when you stand on one leg that you cannot help but squeeze your toes downwards and continually correct your arch position in order to remain upright and balanced. Once this becomes an easy exercise while done on a flat surface, you can make it more difficult by placing a soft object, such as an old pillow or similarly unstable item, under your foot. (You can purchase specific wobble boards or discs for this purpose.) You can also close your eyes to remove visual cues that help you balance, if you want to add difficulty. As with several others, this exercise can be done daily while you are doing something else, like brushing your teeth, so you do not need to set aside extra time. As the general wisdom is to brush your teeth for two minutes using an electrical toothbrush or three minutes with a manual toothbrush, alternate your legs every 30 seconds while brushing for the desired time. To further work on your balance and coordination, try alternating your hands as you brush your teeth every time you swap legs.

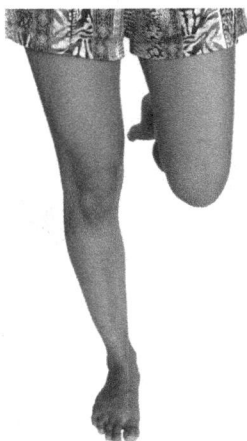

Single leg balance

2. Larger movement – extrinsic muscle exercises

For the following larger-movement, extrinsic foot-muscle-strengthening exercises, I recommend doing them two to three times per week with a rest day in between, e.g., Monday, Wednesday, and Friday. Aim for three sets of between 10 to 15 repetitions, concentrating on the timing: two seconds up, two seconds pause at the top, and two seconds down to the ground or below the level of a step. Doing the exercises over a step is preferable as you garner greater length and activation of the calf muscles, Achilles tendon, and other extrinsic muscles of the feet that are assisting this movement.

The goal with these exercises is eventually to use weights either at home or at the gym, ideally with the guidance of the right practitioner to make sure both lower limb and upper body postures are correct. Doing these exercises initially with only your body weight will give you a great baseline upon which to build, especially if you are a complete beginner to both running and strength training. Make a note to concentrate on the correct technique rather than trying to complete repetitions without full range. Again, if you experience any pain during these exercises, please stop straight away and seek professional advice.

Straight-leg double-leg calf raises

This movement primarily works the calf muscles and Achilles tendon, although it also activates the other assisting plantar flexion muscles and tendons of the foot, in particular the tibialis posterior muscle and tendon, which plays an important role is supporting the medial longitudinal arch of the foot.

If you are new to calf-strengthening exercises, this double-leg version is a great one to start with. I eventually get my patients to do one set of these as a warm-up, once they have graduated to the single-leg versions. If you are new to strength training, you can graduate to the single-leg versions once you can do the three sets of 15 repetitions easily without pulling up sore the next day.

While holding onto a wall, stairwell railing, or something similar, place your heels over a step (or on the ground if a step is not available) with only the front part of your feet (ball of the feet) touching the step. Raise yourself onto your toes over a two-second period, pause at the peak for two seconds, then lower yourself slowly to just below the level of the step over another two seconds. If you are doing this exercise over a step (instead of flat on the floor), you can pause for another two seconds at the bottom. Repeat this movement for 15 repetitions. Rest for 30 seconds between sets. Repeat three times.

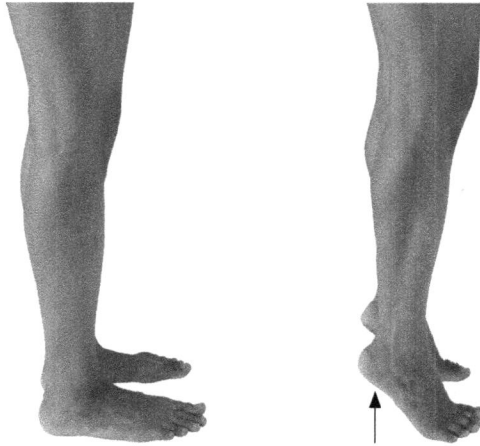

Straight-leg double-leg calf raises

Bent-knee double-leg calf raises

This exercise enables greater activation of the soleus muscle, one of the muscles of the calf. Alternate this version with the straight-knee version, i.e., do one or the other on alternate workout days, e.g., Monday, straight knee; Wednesday, bent knee; Friday, straight knee; Monday, bent knee, etc.

Use the same set-up, movement, timing, sets, and repetitions as the earlier straight double-leg calf raise exercise. The exception is that this time you need to perform the exercise with a slight bend in your knees and maintain this slight bend throughout the whole movement. Pay particular attention as you reach the top of the movement, as a common error is straightening the knees at this point. A good cue is to keep slightly crouched in the knees through the whole movement.

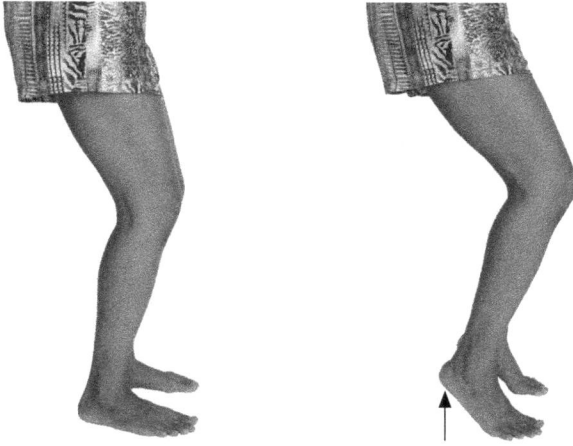

Bent-leg double-leg calf raises

Straight-leg single-leg calf raises

Once you find the double-leg versions relatively easy, you can graduate to these single-leg versions. The set-up for this exercise is the same as the straight-knee double-leg calf raises, except this time you take one foot off the ground which places all of your weight onto the other leg. As before, rise onto your toes over two seconds, pause at the top for two seconds, and then lower yourself towards the ground, or just below the level of the step, over two seconds. Pause for an additional two seconds at the bottom if doing over a step.

I find with runners who have never done these single-leg versions before that the temptation is to speed up and use your body's momentum to rise, particularly as you fatigue. Please remember it is important not to lose form or timing. If you find yourself fatiguing before completing the desired number of repetitions, it is better to reduce the number of repetitions (e.g., 6–8 per leg vs 15) rather than just trying to get through them. You can increase the number of repetitions up to 15 as you become stronger. If lowering the number of repetitions, do still try and complete approximately 30 repetitions in total, e.g., five sets of six repetitions or four sets of eight repetitions (a total of 30–32 repetitions).

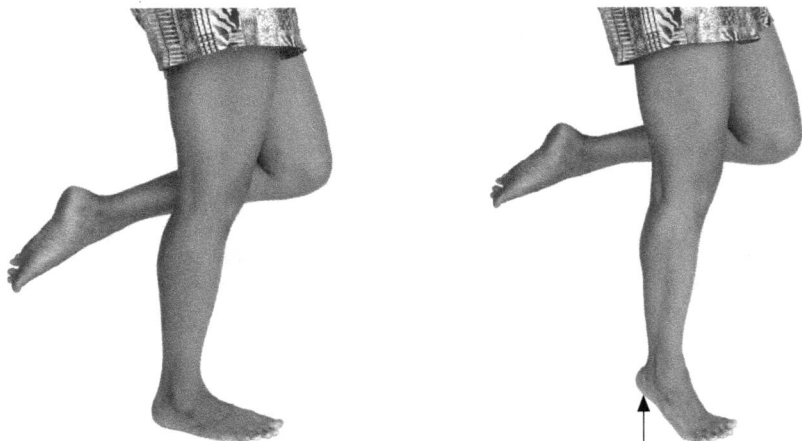

Straight-leg single-leg calf raises

Bent-knee single-leg calf raises

This exercise uses the same set-up as the earlier straight-knee version, but adds a slight bend in the knee (as described in the previous bent-leg double-leg calf raises). Alternate this version with the straight-knee version, i.e., do one or the other on alternate workout days; e.g., Monday, straight knee; Wednesday, bent knee; Friday, straight knee; Monday, bent knee, etc.

Remember not to lose your form or timing. The tendency with this exercise is to sometimes lose form by straightening the knee at the top, especially as you fatigue. Concentrate on keeping the slightly bent position through the whole movement. If you struggle with three sets of 10 repetitions with perfect form, reduce the number of repetitions, still trying to complete a total of approximately 30 repetitions.

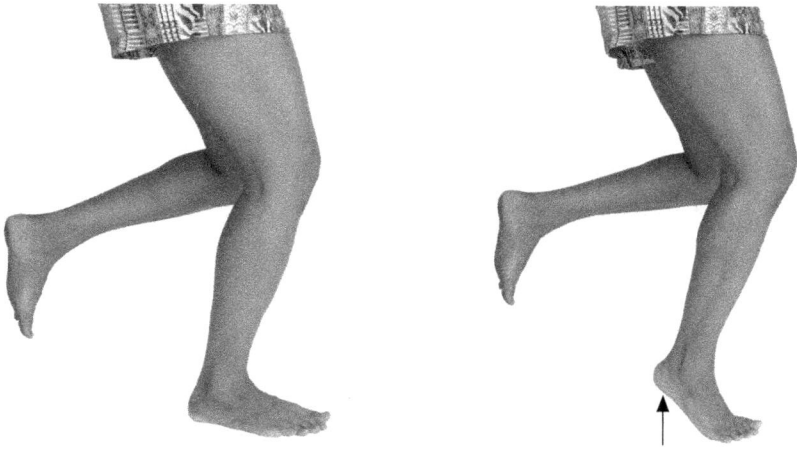

Bent-knee single-leg calf raises

Tip #2

Seek professional advice before choosing running shoes

As noted in chapter 7, there is no clear answer about which category of running shoe (traditional, minimalist, or maximalist) is better for you in terms of preventing injuries. At the end of the day we need to wear something on our feet while running to protect us. Most of us are not hardcore enough to run barefoot on hard, rough surfaces. However, given that there is no clear advantage to be had, we may not need to be as rigid with our shoe selection as was once thought.

The same can be said in terms of podiatrists prescribing specific running shoes for you, as 'despite running shoes being prescribed on the basis of foot morphology (the form, shape, or structure of the foot) for the past 40 years, there is a lack of conclusive evidence that they prevent running related injuries' and that changing running biomechanics through gait re-training may be a better choice than reliance on running shoes to reduce running injury risk.[142]

So, with all of this potentially conflicting information and the plethora of running shoes and their endless differing features, how do you select your running shoes?

There is value in seeking professional podiatry advice to help you cater for your individual circumstances, including your running experience and any running injury history. A professional can respond to your needs, while making sure you understand that whatever is placed on your feet must be comfortable to run in, for reasons discussed earlier in describing the 'comfort filter' paradigm suggested by Nigg et al. (2015).[143] If you want to start using a different type of running shoe, such as a more minimalist model, then a suitably experienced podiatrist will review with you any potential injury risks commonly associated with that particular category, and make sure you put the right measures in place to counter such risks.

Below are seven important considerations that, as a podiatrist, I keep in mind when helping runners choose their shoes:

1. **Goals** – Someone who is a complete beginner and wants to run 10 km per week for fitness is going to have different shoe selection considerations versus a more experienced runner running 80+ km per week and maybe training for their tenth marathon. For example, the more experienced runner usually engages in different running sessions (long runs, tempo sessions, intervals, and speed work) and may run on trail within their cycle, and choose different shoes for the varying sessions. This may help limit wear on running shoes, but the variety underfoot may also be good to help prevent injuries, as discussed in the next tip, #3. As they do more kilometres, they must consider the durability of their running shoes, including monitoring the number of kilometres run in each pair. If they are trialling a new category of shoe, they must make sure they feel 100 per cent comfortable during short runs before using them for long runs. Finally, consideration for what they wear on race day is important, especially allowing enough time to get used to a new, potentially lighter weight, less supportive running shoe leading up to the event.

2. **Running experience** – This is especially important if a runner with no major injury history is contemplating using a traditional lightweight trainer or a minimalist running shoe for the first time. To help decide this, I consider how long they have been running, what sort of distances they run, what types of sessions they do, and the different terrains they train on. Their knowledge about running technique and understanding about cadence is also important. An absolute beginner runner,

for example, might be best served sticking initially to a more traditional running shoe, the benefits of which are discussed in chapter 6, as opposed to a minimalist running shoe. This is especially the case as some of the identified benefits of running in minimalist running shoes (on the more minimal end of the scale, e.g., zero drop) covered in chapter 7, such as landing on the forefoot, do not seem to automatically occur in beginner runners, as previously discussed. A traditional high-mileage running shoe would also be a wiser choice as opposed to a lightweight version, because the added cushioning aims to help protect the body against high-impact forces, especially while becoming accustomed to the increasing running load. In contrast, a more experienced runner, who has slowly built their running load over time, demonstrates great technique, and has considered all aspects of the running-injury prevention picture may be more suited to choosing to incorporate lightweight trainers and more minimalist running shoes as part of their rotation.

3. **Injury history** – This is important to consider as different shoe categories can place more load in certain areas. If a runner has a persistent injury we may look at recommending a particular category of running shoe with features aimed at lessening the load on the affected site. For example, a runner with a long-standing history of Achilles tendinopathy might be advised to wear a traditional running shoe with an elevated heel, as opposed to a minimalist running shoe with a lower heel drop, to ease the load on the Achilles tendon. A runner with a long history of recurring patellofemoral pain might be advised to run in a more minimalist type running shoe which attempts to garner some of the effects of barefoot running. As mentioned previously, in particular, the shorter stride length while barefoot running and potentially running in minimalist shoes may help decrease forces at the knees.

4. **Running-shoe history** – This may shed light on what has and hasn't worked well in the past, including experience with particular categories of running shoes. Inspecting running shoes for wear patterns may guide runners to favour particular features. For example, excessive medial leaning (when viewed sitting on a flat surface) of a running shoe may indicate premature medial wear of the midsole foam. This runner's foot may display over-pronation, and if they are not wearing one already, a running shoe with a medially posted dual-density midsole stability feature might be a better option, as long as it is as comfortable as previous pairs, to achieve longer, potentially less injurious wear out of the shoes.

5. **Current ankle joint range of movement and strength and flexibility of the calf muscles** – If weaknesses in these areas are identified, a more traditional shoe type with an elevated heel to protect these structures might be recommended, at least until the weaknesses are addressed. For example, if a runner has weak, tight calf muscles on testing, a more traditional running shoe with a 10–12-mm heel drop as opposed to a minimalist style running shoe with an 8-mm drop or less would be advisable. Once the runner has met certain strength and flexibility markers, as well as gradually built their running load over time, it may be possible to include lower-pitched minimalist running shoes as part of their rotation.

6. **Foot function and flexibility type** – Observing the way the foot moves through the stance phase of the running gait cycle is important to potentially match certain features of different brands and models within brands. For example, while there is still a lack of evidence to support this in terms of preventing running-related injuries, if your feet do over-pronate, in my experience it is still important to gravitate towards a medially posted stability running shoe, for reasons mentioned already in consideration 4, *as long as it is just as comfortable as its*

neutral counterpart. I know of no evidence to suggest that medially posted stability running shoes will actually cause harm, as long as they are comfortable.

Ascertaining whether a runner has a hypermobile (very flexible) or a hypomobile (rigid) foot type may also determine what other running shoe features are useful. The more flexible your feet are, the more stability and stiffness features are usually recommended to counter over-movement. And the more rigid your feet are, the more flexibility and cushioning features you want that avoid interfering with your foot movement. That said, there are exceptions to this, making it wise to seek in-person advice for your feet.

7. **Foot strike** – Foot strike is important to assess mainly to determine whether certain traditional running shoe features are even considered. You can potentially save weight when selecting your shoes, as stability shoes are traditionally heavier. For example, medially posted midsole stability features are designed to support the foot from heel strike through to toe off, so striking on your forefoot negates the effect. A lighter traditional neutral running shoe or a more minimalist type of running shoe, depending on running experience, may be a better option for runners who forefoot strike. As noted in tip #4, keeping on an eye on wear patterns is important if you forefoot strike in a traditional running shoe, as the front of the midsole may wear faster because it is being used for both impact absorption and propulsion.

Making the final decision

You may have lots of information from a podiatrist, including a number of brand and model recommendations, but you still need to visit a running-shoe store to make your decision.

Your podiatrist's recommendations are never set in stone, because in the end only you can decide what is most comfortable to run in. There are many options, often making the choice overwhelming. To make the process easier, here are four key points to consider when making your decision:

1. **Choose a local running-shoe store vs shopping on the internet** – Let's deal with the elephant in the room. Yes, you can buy running shoes cheaper online, but in my opinion, if you are serious about your running, there is no substitute for your local knowledgeable running-shoe store. They have firsthand knowledge about brands and models. They know which brands tend to fit certain odd foot shapes better, about shoe life expectancy, possess important feedback from other runners, information about changes from previous models, and have experience working alongside podiatrists. These are all important factors to consider and they are the experts at this. I would be lost without their knowledge, help, advice, and the great service they provide for my runners.

2. **Go into a running-shoe store with an open mind** – This is especially true if you are a seasoned runner. Variations exist between brand models each year, and even if a previous brand or model did not feel right before, it doesn't mean it won't now. Conversely, the current season's version of a running shoe brand or model you have been loyal to may no longer feel as good. So, don't make up your mind beforehand. Consider trying on a few models you may have previously disregarded. You might be surprised how comfortable they feel now. Also, don't be afraid to try on something non-traditional (minimalist

or maximalist) to see how it feels underfoot. Ask questions. If you do not currently use non-traditional shoes in your rotation, you might well consider them at a later stage with advice from your podiatrist. See tip #3 for the potential benefits of rotating between different categories of running shoes.

3. **Have your feet measured** – If this is your first serious running shoe, get measured by staff using a Brannock device. It's tempting to assume that the size of your new running shoes should mirror your usual work or casual shoe size. But it can cause blisters, nerve irritations and even long-term toe deformity to wear an ill-fitting shoe. (How to fit your running shoes properly is discussed in more detail further on.)

4. **Try on at least two or three different brands and models and choose the one that feels the most comfortable** – Across their ranges, each brand is trying to achieve similar things in different ways in terms of cushioning, support, and propulsion, making them feel different underfoot. Especially if you are new to running, try on multiple brands and models to assess how comfortable they feel through the entire stance phase of your running gait. Whether or not they fit the shape of your foot comfortably is important, particularly through the width of the toe box. If you have difficulty choosing because they all feel similar, choose the lightest shoes as this helps with running economy. That said, lightness should never surpass cushioning and/or comfort. The running-shoe store staff or an online search will provide each shoe's weight. I provide this for my patients when I am referring for shoes.

Note: You can use these points even if you have not visited a suitably experienced podiatrist for more in-depth recommendations. A reputable running-shoe store will be able to provide you with great recommendations and advice.

Fitting your running shoes properly

It is important that your running shoes are fitted properly to prevent common irritations, especially in the forefoot. Too often I see runners who have worn shoes that were too small for their running life to date.

I find that women's running shoes in particular are often fitted too small, most likely because women fit their running shoes similarly to how they fit their casual shoes, which is right against the end of their toes. This would be OK if the shape of the toe box of all running shoes was more like the shape of your feet, i.e., square. Instead, most running shoes come to a rounded point, so fitting them in this way involves squashing the forefoot and toes.

Fitting your running shoes tightly to the toes also does not allow for any forward drifting of the feet inside the shoe. If you run on undulating road or a steep downhill trail, too tightly fitted shoes can lead to blisters, toenail bruising, and even the loss of toenails on long runs. The tight fit causes the toes to be bunched together in the shape of the toe box. Our toes are quite malleable and can put up with a bit of pressure, but sustained pressure can potentially lead to long-term deformation: claw toe, bunions, and nail deformities. Short-term pressure can cause problems such as in-grown toenails, peripheral digital and interdigital blisters, corns, and callouses. Another problem with fitting your running shoes tightly to your toes is that with a decrease in length there comes a decrease in width. This can compress the nerves that run between the metatarsal bones and into the toes, potentially leading to a common forefoot nerve condition called a Morton's neuroma (see appendix 1).

Below are six key fitting points to consider when you try on running shoes in a store:

1. Always stand to test the size of the running shoes, because your feet lengthen and expand when you stand.

2. Ideally wear the socks or ones very similar to what you usually run in.

3. Have an adult thumb's width between the longest toe and the end of the shoe's toe box. This may mean you have to go 1–1.5 sizes longer than the actual length of your foot. For most, this will be a larger size than what you are used to for your casual shoes, so don't be alarmed. It is better for your feet, and you will get used to it.

4. You should be able to feel both sides of the widest parts of your forefoot within the toe box, but the foot should not bulge out the sides; neither should you be able to pinch material on either side.

5. Once the laces are tied, the eyelets should be evenly aligned width-wise to the opposing eyelets and you should not be able to see either edge of the tongue, a sign that the running shoes are too narrow for your feet.

6. There should not be any slipping of your heels up and down as you do your test run in the store. If they do slip, they may be too big and/or the laces have not been tied tightly enough. If the size has been deemed as appropriate but the heels still slip, try a special lacing technique called the ankle lock, described further on, that can sometimes help with this. Failing this, try on a similar running shoe that may have a better heel counter shape and design for your feet. This is one of many situations where a local running-shoe store can help you.

A few running-shoe fitting hacks

Not all feet are easy to fit, even if you have followed the fitting points above. Moreover, you may have already forked out considerable expense for new running shoes that may have not been fitted properly in the first place and cannot afford to purchase new ones straight away. This is where the following running-shoe fitting hacks may come in handy.

Volume lacing

This can create extra width and breathing space in the upper for your forefoot, especially good for those extra-wide feet or if your current running shoes were fitted slightly too narrowly. I often demonstrate this to patients suffering from a Morton's neuroma and/or intermetatarsal bursitis to allow a little extra room to decompress the forefoot.

To create more volume in the front of the running shoe, unlace the shoe entirely and start the re-lace one eyelet up from the lowest eyelets.

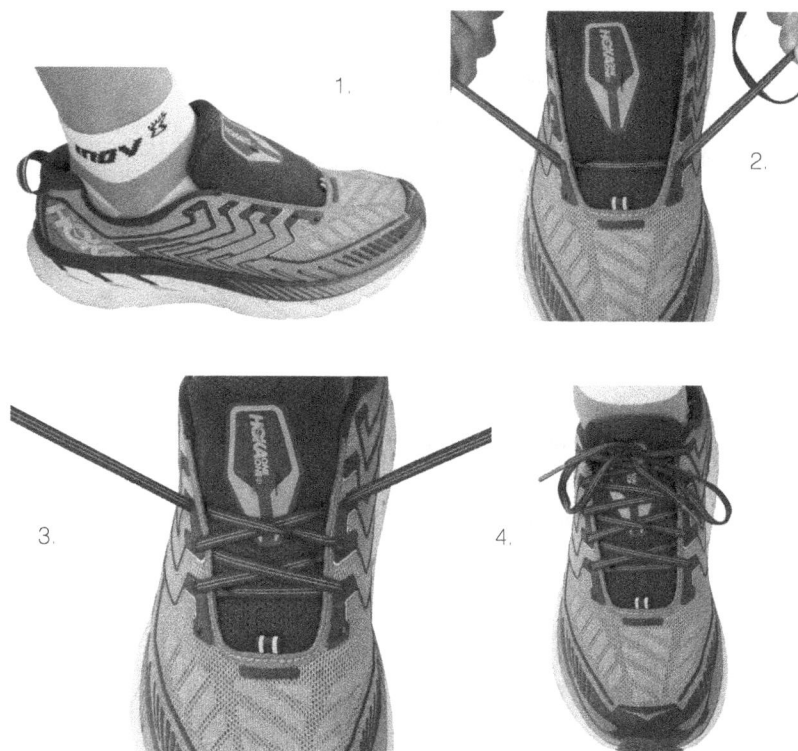

Volume lacing – missing the first eyelets

Another area where this volume lacing can come in handy is in the middle of the laces section, especially if a runner has very high arches and suffers from discomfort possibly due to compression on the top of the foot. To decide where to create volume, feel for the highest part of the arch and then bypass lacing the eyelets that align with this area.

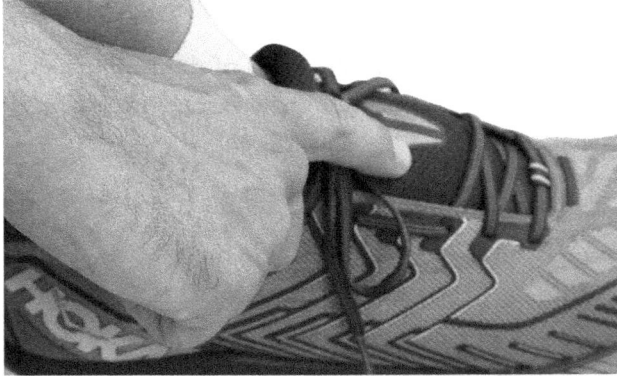

Volume lacing – middle of lace area

Ankle-lock lacing

This is a handy lacing technique for runners who may have wide feet but narrow heels. Such a runner may have had to push the boundaries of the thumb rule lengthwise to find enough width in the shoe, resulting in the shoe possibly being slightly too big and slipping up and down at the heels. As the name suggests, this technique locks the ankle as well as the heel into the shoe.

I also recommend this technique when trying to get as much support out of the upper of a running shoe as possible. The upper can act as a supportive brace whose features we can use to further complement the other supportive parts of running shoes, as well as foot orthoses, if used.

Start by using the 'misplaced' eyelet holes that lie adjacent to the top eyelets and make a loop on the same side.

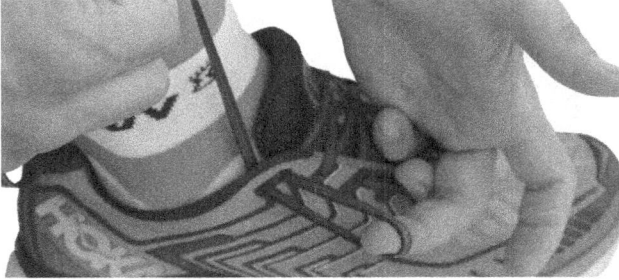

Looping same side

Keeping the loops open, thread each end of the laces back through the opposite loops.

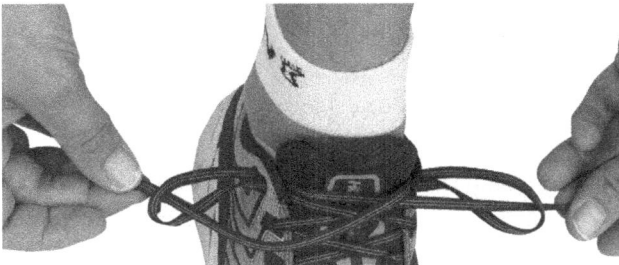

Crossing opposite

Grabbing both lace endings at the same time, pull them up to tighten. While keeping the tension, pull them back down to lock. Repeat this action a couple of times until the laces around the ankle feel firm but not so firm that they are uncomfortable. Always finish pulling down and then tie off the laces as normal.

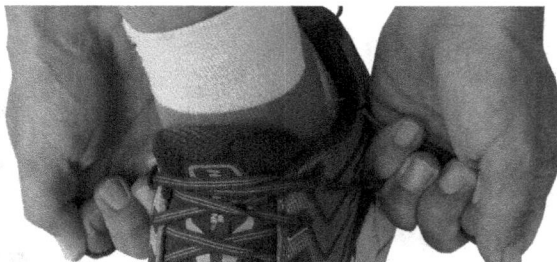

Moving laces up and down

Women can wear men's running shoes for greater width

One of the main differences between men's and women's running shoes is the range of larger sizes available in the men's versions (women's running shoes often finish at size US 11W), different widths and, of course, colours. There are a few brands that do offer specific women's versions, for example, models that have a narrower heel for a better women's anatomical fit. A handy trick for women with very wide feet who have difficulty finding adequate women's sizes is to try on a same length European size in the men's version to see whether they feel more comfortable. The ankle-lock technique, described above, may be necessary if there is any slipping at the heels. If you have any concern at all about colours, you may be able to find a suitable men's shoe in black.

Don't forget about running socks

Socks are an important part of your running gear. The right ones manage skin moisture, protect you from blisters and callouses, and potentially provide added protection from impact forces.[144]

Technical running socks differ from standard cotton socks in that they are made out of a blend of different synthetic (man-made) fibres that have been engineered to include different properties desirable for performance, such as water resistance, wicking, thermal insulation, anti-microbial resistance, reduced weight, cushioning, and reduced friction.[145] Other important features include durability, maintaining their shape when wet, machine washability, quick drying, and being odour resistant.[146]

The synthetic fibres of acrylic and polyester are commonly used in running socks and, in particular, display superior water-resistant and wicking properties.[147] Cotton socks are very good at absorbing moisture; however, they do not wick very well or allow enough transfer of moisture to the shoe upper for gradual evaporation into the outside environment.[148] As a result, when wet, cotton socks can bunch and stretch, while synthetic fibre socks are more likely to retain their shape, cushioning, and resiliency.[149]

A natural fibre that is commonly used in running socks is Merino wool, which is a specialised wool yarn. It has a much finer core diameter per fibre than normal wool, giving it a softer feel and more air space for moisture movement. It is considered superior by manufacturers to any synthetic fibres for insulation and wicking. Socks composed of primarily Merino wool have also been suggested to be the best at shock attenuation.[150]

Although technical running socks are expensive, mainly because manufacturing involves piecing multiple fabrics together, my advice is to spend your money on good socks. This is mainly to help prevent the dreaded blister, but also to help improve your running experience, especially comfort-wise. When deciding, don't be afraid to initially purchase two or three different brands so that you can gauge which are the most helpful and comfortable, if you do suffer from blisters.

Tip #3

Use a variety of running shoes

Apart from it being fun to break up the potential monotony of running training sessions, there may be other benefits to be gained from running in more than one type of running shoe. Each running shoe brand has a different way of trying to achieve similar things – cushioning, support, and propulsion. Because of the variety of materials that they use, the different firmness and blends of foam in the midsoles, the variation in systems of support and stability, as well as the different heel to toe drop heights, your feet and lower limbs react differently while running in them.

The variation introduced by using different running shoes at different times could potentially further break the repetitive nature of running and have running injury prevention benefits. One study, by Malisoux, Ramesh, Mann, Seil, Urhausen & Theisen (2015), showed that runners who reported using different pairs of running shoes during the observation period had a 39% lower risk of running injuries when compared to runners using only one pair of shoes. They did note that further study was required on whether reduced running-related injury risk could specifically be 'ascribed to the alternation of different shoes characteristics, such as midsole densities, structures or geometries'.[151]

There is not one specific way to rotate running shoes. Traditionally, high-mileage cushioned (stability or neutral) running shoes are used for long runs and lightweight running shoes for shorter running sessions that include intervals, tempo, and speed sessions. You might also incorporate a maximalist running shoe as your long-run shoe. Don't be afraid to rotate your shoes, while continually assessing your recovery and any painful areas that arise. And make sure you cover all the other areas of injury prevention.

I find that introducing a new type of running shoe that you have never worn before is best done during a shorter run, enabling you to gain confidence in the comfort and allow your body to adapt to the different variables under your feet. Indeed, there is some evidence to suggest that plantar pressures are higher in new shoes possibly due to their lack of flexibility, and it has been recommended that new running shoes should be broken in 'slowly, using them for mild physical activity'.[152]

If you are just beginning your running journey, using only one type of shoe is a fine way to proceed. Buying more than one pair of running shoes is a bigger investment and you want to make sure you are going to run long term before committing too much financially.

Below are two tables with examples of how to rotate your running shoes. These examples are based on running four days per week and using two or three different categories of running shoe. I have not included minimalist shoes in either table because, as mentioned previously, it is important that you seek professional advice before considering incorporating this type of running shoe.

Rotating between two pairs of shoes

	Monday Short recovery run	**Wednesday** Intervals	**Friday** Tempo	**Sunday** Long run
Traditional lightweight		✓	✓	
Traditional high-mileage	✓			✓

Rotating between three pairs of shoes

	Monday Short recovery run	Wednesday Intervals	Friday Tempo	Sunday Long run
Traditional lightweight		✓ Rotate next session with traditional high-mileage	✓	
Traditional high-mileage		✓ Rotate next session with traditional lightweight		✓ Rotate next session with maximalist
Non-traditional maximalist	✓			✓ Rotate next session with traditional high-mileage

Tip #4

Know when to replace your running shoes

As mentioned earlier, the main purposes of the midsole of your running shoes is to cushion against impact forces, as well as provide energy return during the propulsion phase. Any increase in the kilometres you run involves an increase in the number of running steps and therefore a gradual decrease in the impact-dissipating ability of the running shoes. For example, a study by Cook, Kester & Brunet (1985) showed that identical running shoes worn by two volunteers retained approximately 70% of their initial shock absorption after 800 kilometres.[153] Even though running-shoe foam and technology have evolved a little since 1985, this study shows that foam wears in regards to its shock absorption ability, something that has been suggested might play a role in running injuries.[154] Knowing when to replace your running shoes is clearly important.

Common advice given by podiatrists is to replace your high-mileage traditional running shoes somewhere between 600 and 800 kilometres. However, this can differ slightly amongst runners, with wear time varying on either side of these distances, depending on several factors.

The foam density placed into a running shoe is chosen to balance being soft enough to provide cushioning with being firm enough to remain responsive and propulsive underfoot. It also needs to maintain a decent memory close to its original shape for some distance. There is, however, a trade-off between these elements. The softer the running shoe's midsole foam is, the quicker it tends to lose its memory, and the faster it will wear.

Each brand uses different types and blends of foam in their midsoles, which impact how long the running shoes last. Different brands and models can feel fantastic out of the box, yet don't retain the same feel after a few hundred kilometres, while other brands may not feel as fantastic straight out of the box but feel more consistent well above the 500-km mark in terms of cushioning and response under foot.

The wear of a running shoe's midsole can also depend on an individual's stature, foot strike pattern, and foot function. For example, a heavier individual is going to compress foam more on each foot strike versus a lighter runner wearing the exact same shoe and size. Also, a runner who is a forefoot striker, for example, will compress the front of the running shoe more often, as they use it for both impact and propulsion. Traditional running shoe outsoles (made from blown and/or carbon rubber) that protect the softer midsole foam are also not structurally designed for impact in this area (forefoot), and I find premature wear (less than 500 km) in a traditional high-mileage running shoe is not uncommon. This can be compared to a heel striker who uses different parts of the shoe for impact (heel) and propulsion (forefoot).

Excessive movement with either over-pronation (rolls in too far from what is considered ideal) or over-supination (rolls out too far) during the different stages of the stance phase of running gait can potentially lead to different areas of your running shoes wearing faster than others. For example, as mentioned earlier, if an individual severely over-pronates, which loads the medial side of the running shoe more often, this can lead to quicker wear of this part of the midsole. In contrast, if a runner over-supinates and rolls to the outside of the shoe more often, this can cause faster wear on the lateral part of the midsole. A good test to see if this is happening to your shoes is to place them on a flat desk or bench and see if the shoe leans excessively towards one side or the other. If either of your shoes does this, they may be worn out, or close to that state. As mentioned previously, this may be an important observation by a podiatrist who may use this premature wear to help them guide you towards a different category of traditional running shoe, i.e., one that has midsole features that may help prolong the stability and abnormal wear of the midsole. For example, for an over-pronator, medial posting stability features built into the midsole may reduce the compression of the foam and therefore hold its ground for longer.

Another consideration is what the running shoe may have been designed for. For example, you can't expect a traditional lightweight trainer to last as long as a traditional high-mileage running shoe, because it typically doesn't have as much foam or stiffer stability features built into the midsole. I find that a lightweight trainer typically wears between 400 and 600 km on average, compared to the 600 to 800 km of a traditional high-mileage running shoe, depending, of course, on the points discussed earlier.

Wear patterns on the outersole rubber of both road- and trail-running shoes can indicate running shoes that are worn out or wearing unevenly. Typically, if your running shoe has begun to wear through to the midsole layer and the outersole lugs are flat, most likely the midsole is worn out.

Lastly, a common worry of running patients is that their running shoes are wearing at the lateral part of the back of the heels. Unless the wear is significantly different from one shoe (right or left) to the other, this wear is normal – this is the common strike zone for heel strikers. If there is significant difference, this could indicate an issue on one limb's kinetic chain, such as tightness or restriction of movement during the swing phase of the running gait. If significant difference is evident, this should definitely be assessed by a suitably experienced podiatrist or other health professional.

Tip #5

Use casual and work shoes to your advantage

An often-overlooked area in helping to prevent running injuries, in particular by aiding recovery between running sessions, is the role of work and casual shoes.

These are the shoes we spend most of our time wearing. If they are inadequate, they can place undue stress on various soft tissue structures, particularly in the feet. While possibly not directly causing an injury, they can potentially lead to fatigue in the feet and legs, an accumulation of which, when combined with an increasing running load, could increase injury risk.

Both the multifactorial causes of running injuries and the lack of studies to date relating to work or casual shoes means all of this is theoretical – supposition. This tip simply incorporates common sense advice to help you make smarter decisions about what you place on your feet every day.

The following are four examples of work and casual shoe mistakes I commonly see, and advice on how to counteract their ill effects.

1. High heels

The daily use of high heels of two or more inches can potentially, long term, shorten the calf muscles and Achilles tendons. The elevated position of the heel, which places the ankle into plantar flexion (foot pointing down), also puts the forefoot, ankles, knees, pelvis, and lower back into less desirable functional positions while standing and walking.

Running involves the ankle bending in the opposite direction (dorsiflexion) during late midstance. As a result, the two extremes could lead to excessive stretching strain of shortened, tight calf muscles and Achilles tendons caused by high heels, and contribute to a running injury if measures are not taken to counteract the shortening effect.

Wearing high heels also increases pressure through the forefoot, especially on the metatarsal phalangeal joints. Because of the heel's elevated position, the toes are bent significantly, reducing their weight offloading ability and exposing the metatarsal heads to greater load. The plantar plates, joint ligaments, and capsules (as detailed in appendix 1) are also placed into a vulnerable, stretched position. High-heeled shoes are also often not very well cushioned, offering little protection from hard surfaces. This constant forefoot load, combined with high running load, may contribute to common conditions such as metatarsalgia, bunions, sesamoiditis, plantar plate strains, tears and ruptures, and metatarsal and sesamoid bone stress fractures.

If high heels must be worn daily as part of a work dress code, there are several solutions to help to avoid the shortening of the calf muscles. The first is to wear lower heels, or to wear lower heels whenever possible; e.g., have both types of shoes available in your office. The second is to remove your shoes whenever you are seated and stretch your calf muscles. Place the front of your feet onto the edge of a thick book or similar – better still, a calf-stretching wedge easily purchased online – and drop your heels over the edge. Alternating high-heel wearing with joggers wherever possible is a particularly useful thing to do (if you can bear the look). Finally, incorporating specific calf stretches into your daily routine is beneficial, as is having regular weekly or fortnightly massages that target the calf muscles.

2. Women's flats

Going too low at the heel of a shoe can also cause problems, because wearing flats places the calf and Achilles tendon on a constant stretch. You may get away without suffering an injury to these structures if you are relatively sedentary, but if you combine wearing flats with a high running load, this could contribute to conditions such as Achilles tendinopathy and plantar fasciopathy. Flats also have little to no cushioning, and walking around on hard surfaces exposes the body to increased impact forces.

Ideally, select footwear that has a slightly elevated (no more than an inch), cushioned heel which will help de-load those soft tissue structures. A broad heel base is preferred over a narrow one for more surface area contact with the ground, giving you greater stability.

3. Men's and women's casual shoes

Men do not avoid this risk either, and sometimes I recommend changing men's casual footwear habits as part of their overall treatment plan. A typical example involves wearing flat, non-cushioned Converse Allstar-type casual shoes. These have the same effect as the above-mentioned women's flats.

Hyper-flexible casual shoes can also do harm. Although some of these may be extremely cushioned and soft, the foot may have to work harder during walking gait, and that extra work may contribute to overall fatigue in the feet and lower limbs. This is especially true for runners with a hypermobile flat-foot type. When this is combined with a high running load, it could contribute to a running injury.

Luckily, there are some casual shoe options for both sexes that have decent structure to them.

When testing to see if casual or work shoes have good structure, check for these six features:

1. A firm heel counter that ideally does not fold in, which helps support the rearfoot.
2. Resistance to twisting through the midsole, which helps support the structures in the midfoot.
3. The shoe only bends where the toes bend and resists bending, which helps support both the structures in the midfoot and in the forefoot.
4. The shoe has only a slightly elevated heel (no more than one inch).
5. There is a midsole cushioned layer to protect the foot from walking impact forces.
6. Ideally, the shoe has a lacing or a strap system that holds the foot in place as firmly as possible.

4. Thongs/flip flops

Traditional thongs (flip flops) are flat and have a similar effect on the foot as flats and certain other flat casual shoes. They have the added disadvantage of potentially altering our walking gait pattern. Because they are typically loose and do not have a heel or midfoot strap to grip the feet, we need to 'flick' our foot up more than usual in order to keep the thong on. This can cause overstriding, which increases walking impact forces in the feet and the rest of the lower limbs. We also use the muscles at the front of our lower leg that lift our foot and toes more often, so as to keep loose thongs in place, which can lead to muscle overuse.

In hotter climates it can be very hard to avoid wearing thongs, especially as many of us use them as our easy, go-to slip-on shoe. If you are going to use them, especially while engaging in running training, choose what are called orthotic thongs. These feature an elevated heel, added cushioning, a stiffer-to-bend sole, a firmer-fitting forefoot strap, and arch support. If you are happy to wear a sandal with a heel strap and midfoot strap with similar features to the orthotic thongs, this is even better.

The 80/20 shoe rule

As I consistently explain to many of my patients (mostly women), I will never stop you from wearing your favourite shoes. (This is usually right after I get dirty looks from trying to recommend what are described as 'ugly grandma shoes'.)

Early in my career I decided that what was important was to put in place what I call the '80/20 shoe rule', based on the Pareto principle. This simple rule makes it easy to understand the importance of wearing good shoes for your feet more often.

According to this rule, you should wear a really comfortable, supportive pair of shoes 80 per cent of the time, whether you are at work, home, or carrying out weekly chores. The other 20 per cent of shoe wear time is saved for those important meetings and/or special occasions where you can wear what you like without potentially contributing to your risk of injury. There may be some cases, such as people who are recovering from an injury, for whom this rule does not apply. Indeed, you may need to wear a pair of traditional running shoes more often during your recovery period.

In terms of the best shoe you should be wearing 80 per cent of the time, of course it's your traditional running shoes. They have all the right features, including cushioning, bend and torsional stiffness, stability, and an elevated heel, to help keep your feet and lower limbs protected and rested from hard surfaces.

Wearing your traditional running shoes most of the time may not be possible, which is when it can become more difficult to choose comfortable and supportive dress shoes. However, there are definitely better options available. Take what you have learned here regarding the cushioning and supportive features of traditional running shoes and replicate these features as closely as possible. Also, follow the six important casual shoe features identified above. It might not sound very attractive, but a number of work and casual shoe brands try to meet the requirements of support and comfort while still being relatively fashionable. Your local podiatrist can provide more definitive advice on what particular brands you should seek and where to purchase them.

Conclusion

I am sure by now you will have come to appreciate that the foot is complex in terms of both structure and function and contains a number of structures that can be injured directly from running load.

The roles of feet and running shoes should not be considered in isolation. Especially when trying to reduce your running injury risk, there are a number of factors that need to be considered, and it is important to tick as many of the boxes as possible. Fewer injuries means more running, or at least suffering less down time from training, and as long as your program is well thought out, your running performance should improve.

As we have seen, there is also a great deal of ambiguity about exactly what is best, especially when it comes to some of the injury prevention topics discussed in this book. For example, according to research, there is no preferred foot strike pattern or better category of running shoe to help prevent running injuries. Because of this, it is hard to define precisely what the best choice is for you, personally.

So where does this leave us?
Actually, it leaves us in a very good position.

Because there is no *one* solution, you have the ability to build more injury prevention variation into your running. Variation is an important part of any running program and breaks up the repetitive nature of running. It may involve varying each running session (e.g., intervals, tempo sessions, long runs, speed sessions), varying the terrain (e.g., trail vs road vs track sessions) or even incorporating different sports into the mix, particularly ones that involve changes of direction (e.g., touch football, oz tag, basketball, soccer). In doing this, you recruit different muscles and tendons, as well as move your joints in different ways.

Changing the part of your foot that strikes the ground (heel or forefoot), alternating the category of running shoe (traditional, minimalist, or maximalist) you wear, and even running barefoot once in a while are all great ways to vary your running conditions. Each variable alters the forces placed on different structures in the feet and lower limbs. If done wisely, and with guidance, you can make your body stronger, more resilient to injury, and break up the repetitive nature of running.

I hope this information I have provided has been helpful, in particular concerning some of the contentious topics on which I have tried to provide clarity. I also hope you can incorporate some of the healthy running foot tips I have outlined into your running life. These have worked well for my patients over the years and I hope you can benefit from them too – now and down the road.

Appendix 1

Musculoskeletal structures of the foot

The following is designed to highlight the main structures of the foot, the important role each structure plays, how injuries can occur, and commonly associated conditions. It is by no means an in-depth anatomical or physiological lesson. Instead, I have tried to make what can be complex information simpler to understand, so you can better appreciate the complexity of the feet.

Bones

Without the bones that make up our skeleton, our bodies would collapse in a mound of soft tissue mess. Our bones anchor the forces applied by muscles and tendons to allow our bodies to remain upright and move. Bones also protect our vital organs. In total, we have **206** bones in our body, just over a quarter of which (**52**) make up our feet.

Bones are a hard form of connective tissue that comprises the majority of our skeleton. They consist of an organic component (the cells and matrix) and an inorganic, or mineral, component. The matrix contains a framework of collagenous fibres impregnated with a mineral component, mainly calcium phosphate (85%) and calcium carbonate (10%). This is what makes bone rigid.[155]

Bone can be considered a metabolically active organ that goes through continual remodelling throughout our lifespan. Cells, called osteoclasts, remove old mineralised bone while other cells, osteoblasts, build new bone. This remodelling serves to adjust bone architecture to meet our changing mechanical needs and helps to repair micro damage in the bone matrix, preventing the accumulation of old bone.[156]

Changing mechanical needs include any increase in the amount of running load you may do to prepare for an upcoming longer-distance event. Bone can weaken, and a bone stress injury may occur if you do not allow yourself adequate time to increase the mechanical load when preparing for such an event gradually. Bone injuries in the form of microscopic cracks or even a stress fracture can occur, especially when there is too sudden and great a change in intensity and distance while running.[157] Changes in running shoes and training surface may also be risk factors, particularly if impact forces aren't sufficiently dampened.[158]

Damage from running can also occur in those who are more susceptible to stress fractures due to low bone density. Take, for example, the syndrome called 'female athlete triad'. This condition involves low energy availability (due to low calorie intake), amenorrhoea (absence of menstrual periods in women of reproductive age), and osteoporosis (when bones become weak and fragile).[159] In female athletes who suffer from one of these factors in the triad, the risk of stress fracture can be 2.4 to 4.9 times higher. There is also increased risk of a stress fracture later in life.[160]

The most common site for a stress fracture in the lower limbs caused by running is the tibia. Medial tibial stress syndrome (MTSS), also known as shin splints or tibial periostitis, can be difficult to distinguish from a stress fracture.[161] However, MTSS typically occurs over the medial posterior edge of the tibia and is felt during exertional activity (e.g., running) as opposed to a stress fracture, which is frequently felt during day-to-day activities.[162]

Another common stress injury location in the foot related to running is the navicular bone.[163] It is important to diagnose a stress injury in this location as parts of this bone have poor blood supply, putting them at risk of non-union. If this occurs, the whole bone can start to deteriorate or break down, and lead to avascular necrosis (bone death).

Joints

A joint is where two or more bones come together to facilitate body movement. Joints are classified both structurally and functionally.

In structural terms, joints are defined by how they are held together – by fibrous connective tissue (fibrous joint), cartilage (cartilaginous joint), or by a fluid-filled joint cavity (synovial joint).

Functionally, joints are defined by the amount of mobility allowed, including synarthrosis (immobile), amphiarthrosis (slightly moveable), and diarthrosis (freely moveable). Depending on their location, fibrous joints can be synarthrosis or amphiarthrosis, as can cartilaginous joints. All synovial joints are considered, functionally, as diarthrosis joints.

Joints in the feet are all synovial.[164] A synovial joint involves freely moving connections between two or more bones. It provides smooth and coordinated movement of these bones as the actions of muscles and tendons apply forces that move the body. Synovial joints can be further categorised depending on their number of axes of motion: uniaxial (movement in one plane), biaxial (movement in two planes), or multiaxial (movement in all three of the planes of movement). The three planes of movement, which are discussed in chapter 1, are the sagittal, frontal, and transverse planes.

To allow this smooth and co-ordinated movement, as well to provide stability and protection from various loading stresses, synovial joints are made up of several parts:

Joint capsule – This part is vital for the functioning of synovial joints. It seals the joint space, keeping lubricating synovial fluid in position; provides passive stability by limiting joint movement; provides active stability via its proprioceptive nerve endings; and may also form articular surfaces for the joint.[165] It varies in thickness according to the stress to which it is subject, is locally thickened to form capsular ligaments, and may also incorporate tendons.[166] Injuries to the joint capsule can lead to joint laxity and constriction of and/or adhesion to surrounding structures.[167]

The joint capsules of the metatarsal phalangeal joints (ball of the foot joints) can be injured by running. These joints are where the metatarsal bones articulate with the proximal toe bones (proximal phalanges). During propulsion, this area is placed under a large amount of load, especially just before toe-off.

Articular cartilage – This highly specialised connective tissue of synovial joints forms a smooth surface on the opposing bones of the joint. Its main function is to provide a smooth, lubricated surface for articulation in order to facilitate the transmission of loads with low friction.[168] It can also, in most cases, withstand highly repetitive loads, demonstrating little or no evidence of damage or degenerative change.[169] One problem with articular cartilage, however, is that it does not have a blood or nerve supply, which is one reason why it does not heal or repair well when damaged.

Aside from specific trauma, one way in which damage can occur to this connective tissue is by repetitive stress, such as the stress caused by running. A gradual wear of the articular surface can lead to a condition called osteoarthritis, which is the most common disease affecting joints of the human body.[170]

One joint of the foot where osteoarthritis is particularly prevalent is the big toe joint, in part due to the load placed on it during walking and running.[171] Other causes and predisposing factors include joint disease, family history, repetitive trauma, flat feet, excessive pronation, and excessive tension of the plantar fascia.[172] Osteoarthritis in the big toe joint can manifest as marked pain within the joint and reduced functional ability.[173]

Ligaments – These are dense bands of fibrous connective tissue that connect bones in the musculoskeletal system.[174] Ligaments cross joints that have both wide ranges and small amounts of motion. They function primarily to provide stability for joints when at rest and during normal range of motion.[175] They are viscoelastic, which allows them to stretch under tension and return to their original shape when the tension is removed. The laxity or how stretchy the ligaments are contributes to how flexible or inflexible a person can be. For example, someone who is hypermobile will have very 'stretchy' ligaments.

Damage to ligaments can occur if they are stretched past a certain point, or for a prolonged time. This can lead to an imbalance between joint mobility and joint stability, leading to abnormal transmission of forces throughout the joint. Such transmission can result in damage to other structures in and around the joint.[176] For example, if a runner has a previous history of one or more foot or ankle ligament sprains, the potential instability created by either partial tearing or complete rupture of the ligaments may lead to premature osteoarthritis in the associated joint.

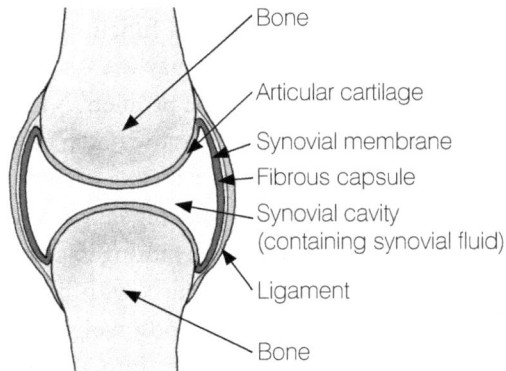

Bone

Articular cartilage

Synovial membrane

Fibrous capsule

Synovial cavity
(containing synovial fluid)

Ligament

Bone

Synovial joint structures

There are several specialised structures in the foot that help to protect the metatarsal phalangeal joints (ball of the foot joints) and adjacent structures. This area is susceptible to high load while running.

Plantar plate – This is a fibrocartilaginous structure made up of type 1 collagen, which is what makes it very strong.[177] Proximally, it is an extension of the plantar fascia with its distal attachments to the base of the proximal toe bone (proximal phalange).[178] Its main roles are to stabilise the metatarsal phalangeal joints while the toes bend during propulsion and to help protect the other joint structures from ground reaction forces.

When we run, this structure is subject to significant tension from the plantar fascia, as well as compression from ground reaction forces, which may cause an increased risk of plantar plate injury.[179] Damage to this structure can take the form of a strain and subsequent tear, which can lead to instability of the joint and pain in the associated joint.[180] Complete rupture can also occur with marked separation, claw toe deformity, and further painful damage to other associated joint structures.

Injury to this structure can often be hard to treat because a runner can present with a number of functional and structural problems in the front of the foot, which may pre-dispose them to a higher risk of damage. One such structural problem is a longer than normal second metatarsal bone (in relation to the first metatarsal bone) which creates a longer lever arm, thereby exerting greater force on the plantar plate of the second metatarsal phalangeal joint with every stride.

Another important contributing factor is non-supportive casual and dress footwear, particularly with heels of two inches or higher. A high-heeled shoe drives body weight onto the metatarsal heads and places the ball of the feet into a more vulnerable toes-bent-up position, further exposing the plantar plate and other joint structures to injury. The impact of wearing high heels may be one reason why the ratio of female plantar plate tears versus males is 10:1.[181]

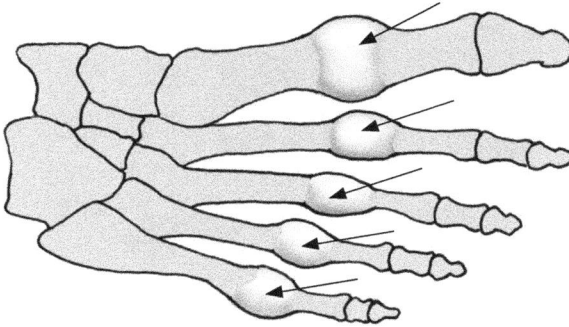

Plantar plate locations

Sesamoid bones – I have singled out these bones in this section on joints because of the important role they play under the big toe joint. Sesamoid bones in general are partially or completely embedded into tendons and act like pulleys, reducing the friction of tendons over joint-forming bones.[182] This increases the tendon's ability to transmit forces. The most well-known sesamoid bone is the patella (knee cap), and also the largest. The patella, which sits within the common tendon for the quadriceps muscles, allows the tendon to glide over the knee joint during movement.

The regular sesamoid bones in the foot are located underneath the big toe joint, although there are rare cases of additional sesamoids in every other joint in the ball of the foot.[183] There are usually two sesamoids, side by side, situated within the medial and lateral heads of the flexor hallucis brevis tendon. The tibial sesamoid bone is the larger of the two and lies more distally than the fibula sesamoid bone, which makes it more susceptible to injury.[184] Not only do the sesamoid bones reduce friction on the tendon they sit in as the big toe bends during propulsion, but they also play a role in protecting the big toe joint from the large ground reaction forces while walking and running. For example, one study showed that forces equivalent to three times our body weight pass through the sesamoid bones during the weight shift of a normal running gait cycle.[185]

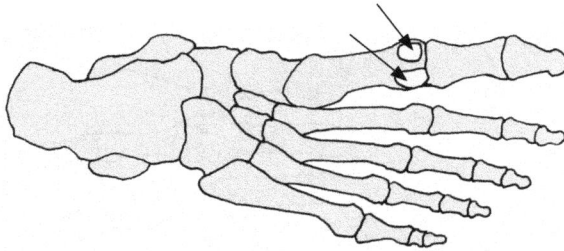

Sesamoid bones in the foot

Subsequent damage to the sesamoid bones can occur as a result of these large forces. A common condition podiatrists see is sesamoiditis, which is inflammation of the sesamoid bones and associated tendons, most commonly due to overload in repetitive movements such as running, jumping, pivoting, and change-of-direction activities.

A condition that you do not want to have misdiagnosed is a sesamoid stress fracture. If a stress fracture does occur, from either trauma or repetitive stress, this disrupts the normal vascular supply to the bone and in some cases can lead to avascular necrosis – bone death.[186]

Skeletal muscles

Skeletal muscles are one of three muscle types in the body, the other two being cardiac muscle (heart muscle) and smooth muscle (muscle that lines organs, particularly the intestines). Skeletal muscles attach to the skeleton to help maintain posture and body position, stabilise bones and joints, and move the body. Skeletal muscles attach to bones via tendons or aponeurosis. They provide the forces required to move the body via the co-ordinated contraction of individual muscle fibres. As such, each skeletal muscle consists of a vast number of muscle cells or fibres that lie parallel to each other. They are linked by connective tissue, which contains blood vessels and nerves.[187]

For the purpose of this book, it is useful to classify the fibres by their characteristics: how fast they contract and how they produce energy. I find that this is the easiest way for runners to understand how each fibre type is used to move the body.

In terms of how they contract, fibres can be broadly classified as 'slow twitch', or Type 1, and 'fast twitch', or Type 2. Fast-twitch fibres are further classified into three major subtypes (Types 2a, 2x, and 2b).[188]

How they produce energy is performed either aerobically (with oxygen) or anaerobically (without oxygen). The ultimate goal is to produce a complex body chemical called adenosine triphosphate (ATP), which provides the energy to drive many processes in the body, including skeletal muscle contraction. Type 1 and Type 2a fibres primarily use oxygen (a process called oxidative metabolism), whereas Type 2x and 2b do not primarily require oxygen (a process called glycolytic metabolism).[189]

Type 1 muscle fibres are the main fibre type utilised in endurance running. The nature of this muscle fibre type enables it to produce more ATP for low-powered contractions over longer periods of time without fatiguing as quickly. This can be compared to Type 2x and 2b muscle fibres, which only produce a limited amount of ATP for muscle contraction in the absence of oxygen and only for a short period of time before fatiguing. Type 1 muscle fibre types play the major role in power activities, such as sprinting and weightlifting. Type 2a muscle fibre is important for activities that require both endurance and power. Indeed, Type 2a is thought to be a Type 2 fibre that specifically adapted for endurance exercise.[190]

Different proportions of the types of muscle fibres are found within each individual person, partly as a result of genetics and partly environmental factors.[191] There are also different proportions of skeletal muscle within distinct muscle groups in each individual's body. For example, the soleus muscle (one component of the calf muscle) predominantly comprises Type 1 fibres whereas the triceps arm muscles are mainly Type 2.[192] These proportions are also adaptable, giving muscle fibres the ability to change and adapt to different uses.[193] For example, endurance training (an environmental factor) can cause a modest increase in the proportion of Type 1 fibres.[194]

The different proportions of muscle fibres also play a role in whether or not an individual excels and/or maybe even prefers particular activities. A number of studies have shown that the muscles of elite athletes exhibit specific and predictable patterns of muscle fibre content according to the sports in which they excel.[195] Thus, Noakes has stated:

> For example, sprinters, jumpers, and weightlifters contain a higher percentage of Type 2 fibres. Middle distance (400 to 1500m) runners, cyclists and swimmers tend to have equal proportions of both Type 2 and Type 1 fibres. In long distance (10km to 42km) runners and cross country skiers, the percentage of Type 1 fibres is higher.[196]

In general, skeletal muscles adapt to endurance exercise, demonstrating an increase in the capacity for aerobic metabolism (oxygen consumption) in all healthy individuals.[197] This capacity is unique to each individual, but also responds to training.[198] Ideally, this training would involve a gradual increase in running load over time to allow this adaptation to occur.

A common running injury involving the skeletal muscle is a calf muscle strain. This is frequently caused by sudden dorsiflexion of the foot at faster than normal running speeds as well as inappropriate body posture, which causes altered muscle length and altered shock absorption.[199] According to Gallo, Plakke & Silvis (2012): 'It has been shown to occur more often in poorly conditioned, middle aged athletes with "thick calves" who engage in strenuous activity.'[200]

Tendons

Tendons attach muscle to bone. They are stiffer than muscles, have greater tensile strength, and can withstand very large loads with minimal deformations.[201] They have a high percentage of collagen (65–80%), making them elastic, capable of resisting high tensile forces, dampening shock, and storing energy when stretched. The basic unit of the tendon is the collagen fibrils.[202] These bunches of fibres are aligned parallel, and exhibit a wavy pattern known as 'crimps'. The ability of the tendon to stretch, store, and release energy, as well as transmit muscle force, is closely related to the tendon collagen fibre's crimp.[203] At rest, they are crimped, but during strain, they become taut, like elastic material. If they elongate too much, they can tear or rupture completely.

Tendons in the body are shaped differently depending on their role. For example, muscles used to perform delicate and precise movements, such as the flexors of the fingers, possess long, thin tendons. In contrast, those that perform actions of power and endurance, such as the quadriceps and calf muscles, have shorter, more robust tendons.[204] For example, the Achilles tendon, the strongest and thickest tendon in the body, resists up to 12.5 times our body weight worth of forces when we run.[205] Because of these high forces, this is one of the most commonly injured tendons during running.[206]

A condition called 'Achilles tendinopathy' (commonly referred to as 'Achilles tendinitis') is a common condition that can occur in runners. It is characterised by a combination of pain, swelling, and impaired performance.[207] The term 'tendinopathy', as opposed to 'tendinitis', is the preferred description for this condition, as there are no inflammatory markers.[208] There are two main categories of Achilles tendinopathy, defined by their anatomical location: insertional and non-insertional.[209] If you suffer from insertional tendinopathy, you feel pain on the back of the heel bone. In non-insertional tendinopathy, you feel pain on the actual tendon, commonly around the mid-portion.

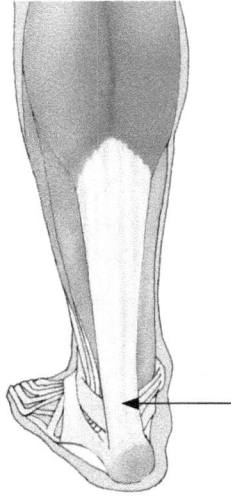

Achilles tendon

Some of the identified causes of Achilles tendinopathy include biomechanical abnormalities of the lower limbs, age, training errors, excessive hill running, training on hard or sloping surfaces, increased mileage, increased repetitive loading, poor shock absorption, and wedging from uneven running-shoe wear.[210] Insufficient heel height of running shoes has also been suggested as a factor.[211]

Fascia

Fascia can be broadly defined as a sheet or band of fibrous connective tissue enveloping, separating, or binding together muscles, organs, and other soft tissue structures of the body.[212] There are three fundamental fibrous connective tissue layers in the human body: superficial fascia, deep fascia, and epimysium.[213] The distinction between these layers is not always clear, since one or more layers can sometimes disappear, or are sometimes strongly connected with each other.[214]

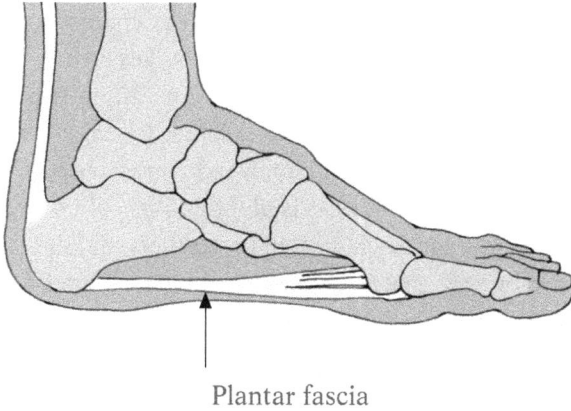

Plantar fascia

The most well-known fascia in the foot is the plantar fascia, which is the deep fascia under the foot. As noted in chapter 1, it has a medial, lateral, and central part, the latter known as the plantar aponeurosis. This thickest central part of the plantar fascia plays an important functional role, supporting the medial longitudinal arch of the foot during weight bearing, helping to absorb impact forces, lifting the arch during propulsion, and providing elastic return energy during the same stage.

If you look at the positioning of the plantar fascia under the foot, you can see why it plays such an important role. It has a proximal attachment at the calcaneus (heel bone) and extends distally into five separate bands that become the digital (toe) sheaths.[215] These bands radiate towards and attach through the plantar plates to the proximal phalanges (proximal toe bones).[216] As noted in chapter 1, together with the bones of the arch of the foot, it forms a triangular truss which helps to prevent the arch from separating and collapsing.[217] During bending of the toes, in both walking and running, the windlass mechanism (see chapter 3) causes the plantar fascia to tighten, contributing to the raising of the medial longitudinal arch.[218]

A common running injury to this structure, and one podiatrists see frequently, is plantar fasciitis. As with tendon damage, it is not an inflammation of the plantar fascia but rather a degenerative pathology, making the term 'plantar fasciopathy' a more appropriate description.[219]

More recent imaging techniques show that the condition affects more than just the plantar fascia (e.g., the heel bone and the surrounding tissue), so the more generalised term 'plantar heel pain' is perhaps more apt.[220] For conditions pertaining to the plantar fascia, however, we will continue to employ the more commonly used term 'plantar fasciitis'.

The location of this condition is identified by pain in the proximal insertion of the plantar fascia into the calcaneus, or heel bone.[221] It is characterised by pain that is worse first thing in the morning and/or after getting up from rest. The pain then eases, but may return after extended periods of walking or standing, or after intense exercise or a running session.

This condition affects 1 in 10 people during their lifetime, with 90% of cases resolving within 12 months with conservative treatment.[222] In relation to the incidence of plantar fasciitis in runners, one systematic review showed that the incidence ranged between 4.5% and 10%, making it the third most frequently experienced running-related musculoskeletal injury.[223] This high incidence is not surprising, given that upwards of three times the body weight worth of forces goes through each foot on each stride and the important supportive, impact-absorbing, functional, propulsive role of the plantar fascia. Some of the risk factors commonly identified with plantar fasciitis in runners include flat feet, high arches, over-pronation, being overweight, calf muscle tightness, intrinsic foot muscle weakness, degeneration of the fat pad under the heel, overuse, training error (e.g., too suddenly increasing the distance, intensity, duration, or frequency of training), and inadequate or worn out running shoes.[224]

Bursa

The bursa is a sac of fluid that provides a buffer between two anatomical structures: bone on tendon and bone on bone. This structure is important because it prevents two structures from rubbing against each other and causing damage.

One example of a bursa protecting a bone and tendon is the retro-calcaneal bursa, located between the antero-inferior wall of the Achilles tendon and the posterior surface of the calcaneus (heel bone).[225] It lies in the region of the Achilles tendon insertion into the calcaneus, and its function is to reduce the friction associated with the tendon's movement in surrounding tissue.[226] Inflammation of the bursa is common, and results in pain, tenderness, and swelling.[227] Retro-calcaneal bursitis is an important differential diagnosis to Achilles tendinopathy, but they often occur in combination.[228]

One example of a bursa that protects bone on bone is the intermetatarsal bursae that lie between the adjacent metatarsal heads in the forefoot. These bursae protect the adjacent metatarsal heads from rubbing against each other, such as the result of compression forces when wearing closed-in shoes. They can be irritated if your running, work, or casual shoes are too narrow and compress the forefoot. With continual compression of the bursae, they can become inflamed, enlarged, and painful. This condition is called 'intermetatarsal bursitis'. A secondary effect of an enlarged bursa is that it can potentially compress a closely coursing digital nerve. It is proposed that this causes an irritation of the nerve and may lead to a condition called 'Morton's neuroma', discussed below.

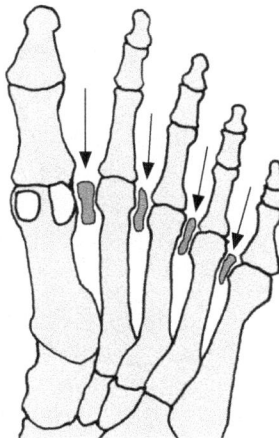

Intermetatarsal bursa locations

Peripheral nerves

The peripheral nervous system includes all neural structures outside the brain and spinal cord. It includes sensory receptors, peripheral nerves and their associated ganglia, and efferent motor endings.[229]

Sensory receptors are specialised to respond to stimuli, i.e., changes in their environment.[230] They are linked to nerves whose stimuli trigger an impulse along the nerves and back to the central nervous system.

Nerves provide the pathways for signals to be transmitted to and from the central nervous system, contracting skeletal muscle as well as providing sensory feedback. There are two types of fibres within a nerve, categorised based on the direction of the signals. Sensory or afferent fibres conduct signals from sensory receptors to the central nervous system (brain and spinal cord). Motor or efferent fibres conduct signals from the central nervous system to muscles and glands. The majority of nerves are mixed, and purely sensory or motor nerves are rare.[231]

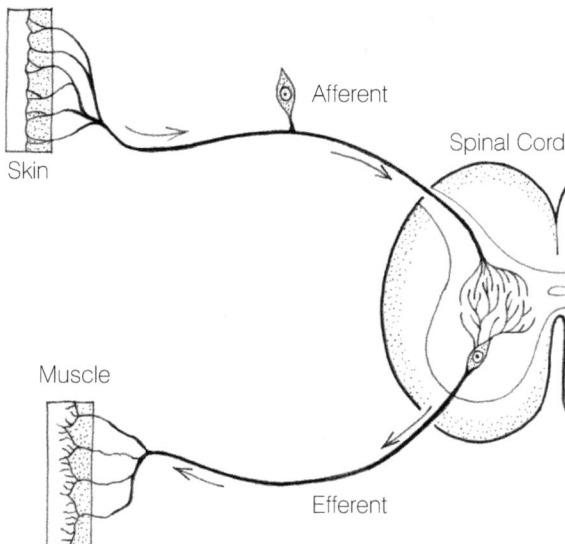

Afferent and efferent fibres

Peripheral motor endings are the terminals where motor nerves innervate voluntary muscles, the muscles we control. They activate each individual muscle fibre by releasing what are called 'neurotransmitters'.

An important peripheral nervous system mechanism is the reflex arc, described as a rapid, predictable motor response to a stimulus. It is unlearned, unpremeditated, and involuntary, built into our neural anatomy.[232] For example, this reflex arc happens during running when our foot and ankle self-correct, following a misstep on an uneven surface.

A common nerve injury is a Morton's neuroma, a thickening of a plantar digital nerve affecting the web spaces of the toes, most commonly the third web space (between the third and fourth metatarsal heads). The complaint is often of a sharp pain, sometimes accompanied by burning, numbness, and tingling in the toes. The irritation can occur suddenly, while walking or running, and can be painful enough to cause the runner to remove the running shoe.

There are various potential contributors to this condition, particularly when it occurs in the most common site, the third web space. These include a naturally larger nerve when compared to the other digital nerves (due to a double origin), inflammation of the intermetatarsal bursa, potential disruption of blood supply due to micro trauma, and mechanical stress caused by an unstable transverse arch.[233]

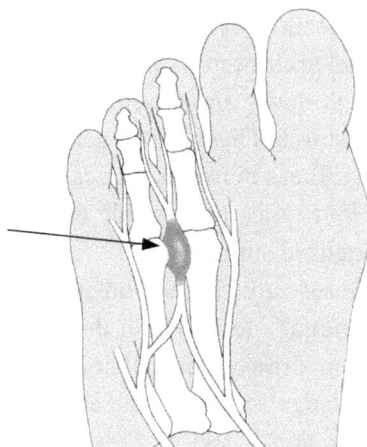

Morton's neuroma

Appendix 2

Foot orthoses

Foot orthoses could easily command their own separate section, rather than being placed in an appendix. As a runner you will inevitably come across them. You may already wear them, have them prescribed by a podiatrist to help treat an injury, see them in a running shoe store, or hear about them from a running friend. There are differing beliefs and strong opinions about them in various running circles. We'll examine what they are, how they are proposed to work and how they do not work, and my personal views on when they should be used.

Foot orthoses (commonly referred to as orthotics) comprise a broad range of in-shoe devices that range from off-the-shelf non-custom devices (non-custom foot orthoses) to prescription, custom-moulded devices (custom foot orthoses). Even within these categories, there are many different types.

Examples of non-custom foot orthoses include the foam (most commonly EVA) and gel arch support insoles that you can purchase over the counter from podiatry and physiotherapy clinics, chemists, sports shops, and shoe stores. These have a generic arch which varies in shape, height, and stiffness between brands. Their main aim is to fit as many different foot types as possible comfortably, while still providing non-individualised support.

Custom foot orthoses are based on the exact shape and dimensions of an individual's foot. When designed by a podiatrist, we combine information drawn from a biomechanical assessment of the individual, knowledge regarding the activity or activities they are going to be used for, and the shoes they'll be used in. Common custom design features include specific arch height, arch positioning, rearfoot tilt angles, rearfoot and forefoot posts, heel cup heights, skives, flares, metatarsal pads, and cut-outs. The podiatrist can also use different types of thermoplastic materials that display different stiffness properties to form the shell of the device.

How do foot orthoses help soft tissue injuries?

The simplest explanation is that they attempt to change the distribution and timing of forces acting under the foot in order to reduce the load on the affected soft tissue. To be successful they need to reduce tissue load to a level where tissue repair can occur.

The exact mechanism of how foot orthoses elicit an effect under the foot is unknown, and popular theories and models need further research and validation.[234] Many of these models involve mechanisms that can be hard to conceptualise without an understanding of complex biomechanics that fall outside the scope of this book.

Foot orthoses do not re-align the skeleton or attempt to make your feet perfectly straight while standing or moving. They have, however, been shown to *alter* movement, as well as the forces acting on and within different parts of the foot and lower leg during walking and running.[235] This is important to understand because there are some non-custom foot orthoses producers who claim their products perfectly align and straighten *all* feet, sometimes by using manipulated before-and-after photos to show the supposed changes. This is misleading. For some individuals, foot orthoses make their feet appear straight, while in others they don't. How straight an individual stands while wearing them should not be considered the goal, or used as a marker of success. People have been incorrectly conditioned to associate mal-alignment of the feet as the cause of running injuries, making it a challenge to explain to an injured patient why using foot orthoses is not done to perfectly align their feet.

Another common misbelief about foot orthoses is that long-term use weakens your intrinsic and extrinsic foot muscles, making you more injury prone. There is no strong evidence for this. As explained, foot orthoses do not hold you perfectly straight and are not aimed at blocking all movement of the foot and ankle while walking or running, so it makes sense that they are also unable to reduce muscle activity to a point that causes the muscles to weaken. They are not a rigid brace locking all of the structures of the foot – the foot and arch still move – which means that intrinsic and extrinsic foot muscles continue to contract.

Interestingly, some studies indicate that wearing foot orthoses can strengthen the intrinsic and extrinsic muscles of flat feet, suggesting they restore the normal length of the muscles, allowing them to function more efficiently.[236] Nonetheless, this potential increase in strength does not automatically translate to a decrease in risk of injury.

Custom versus non-custom

Use of custom versus non-custom foot orthoses in treating foot and lower limb conditions is a hotly debated topic amongst health and medical professionals, mainly due to a lack of strong evidence that one is better than the other in helping to treat certain conditions. Other issues for debate are the high cost of custom foot orthoses for patients as well as the longer manufacturing time, plus associated technological expenses for podiatrists.

One argument for little or no difference between using custom or non-custom foot orthoses in treating various conditions is that the custom foot orthoses used in such studies still need to be standardised between participants, especially in terms of types of materials and features providing support. So, are these truly customised? There are various custom design features that individual podiatrists consider when treating individual patients that cannot be accounted for in a clinical study.

This issue is further complicated, however, by the fact there are no clearly defined evidence-based prescribing guidelines for custom foot orthoses.[237] If you lined up 10 podiatrists and asked them to prescribe custom foot orthoses to help the same injured individual, they could all potentially come up with something different. Such variations include biomechanical measurements, interpretation of those measurements, and the eventual design features chosen. The differences may also be the result of differing theoretical and model beliefs, as well as the individual podiatrist's clinical experience, including past successes and failures when treating conditions using custom foot orthoses.

I find that when deciding between custom and non-custom foot orthoses to treat an injured runner, it comes down to whether or not a non-custom foot orthosis has features that can adequately elicit the desired de-loading of the affected soft tissue structures. If they can, and do it comfortably, then the expense of custom foot orthoses can be avoided, something I consider to be the ideal situation, especially in a running injury case with no long-term history or recurrence.

That said, it is not always easy to find non-custom foot orthoses that are comfortable and achieve the optimal desired effect, whether it's because of an individual's unique arch shape, foot function, or the types of running shoes used. You may need to trial several different pairs to find one that suits.

If a non-custom foot orthosis cannot be found that is comfortable or creates the desired effect, this is not a reason to disregard the use of foot orthoses altogether, especially if they are deemed clinically significant in a treatment plan.

The comfort factor is an important part of the customisation process for compliance. If the correct impression of the foot is taken, the correct biomechanical variables are taken into consideration, and careful consideration is given to placing the right features into the design, custom foot orthoses should be comfortable for most injured runners' feet. If custom foot orthoses are not comfortable, the podiatrist should elicit feedback from the patient and keep making modifications until they are comfortable.

Making a static device for the foot, which changes shape during different stages of the running gait cycle, can be difficult. It may take several adjustments to optimise custom foot orthoses for both comfort and desired effect. If these results cannot be obtained even after these adjustments, a podiatrist may need to reconsider their original prescription and design new custom foot orthoses, hopefully at minimal extra expense to the patient.

I believe that both types of foot orthoses, custom and non-custom, can be useful in helping to treat an injured runner as long as there is a related biomechanical contributing factor. As part of an overall treatment plan, they can play an important role, especially to reduce the stress on affected soft tissue to aid in its repair.

Foot orthoses definitely should not be used to try and 'fix' flat feet, as mentioned in chapter 2, FAQ #1. They cannot do this; neither is there any strong evidence that flat feet or over-pronation are strong predictors of running injury (see FAQs 1 and 2, chapters 2 and 3). As long as all other areas of running injury prevention are covered, it is possible for a runner with flat feet and over-pronation to run without the need for foot orthoses and have no apparent greater injury risk than runners who do not display either.

In terms of the ongoing or long-term use of foot orthoses, I usually reconsider their use once an injury has been fully rehabilitated. There is no problem in using them long term, but in many cases, as long as other areas of running injury prevention have been diligently covered, their use can be discontinued. A suitably experienced podiatrist can give you specific advice on this, depending on your previous injuries and individual circumstances.

The custom foot orthoses process

Capturing the unique characteristics of a patient's feet is traditionally done by making a plaster-of-Paris cast directly from the feet. A more common and often podiatrist-preferred method of capturing the foot now involves using 3D foot-scanning technology. Advantages over traditional plaster casts include less mess, less in-clinic time, less potential human error in manufacturing and reproduction, and greater production speed. The ability to send a positive foot model file electronically to an external foot orthosis laboratory cuts down production and delivery time to the patient. However, there are some foot conditions and characteristics where the traditional method remains superior in terms of capturing a more usable static foot position. Most podiatrists will choose their own method of capturing the feet depending on the goals they want to achieve.

Once a foot model has been obtained, strategic modifications can be made to the model before a thermoplastic (plastic that becomes pliable once heated) sheet is heated and vacuum-pressed onto the model. If a digital foot model has been created, the foot orthosis can be designed directly from the digital model using CAD/CAM (computer-aided design/computer-aided manufacture) software, before it is sent to a milling machine for manufacture. Common thermoplastics include polypropylene, subortholene, and ethylene vinyl acetate. These come in several different thicknesses and densities, depending on the desired outcome and what shoes they will be used with. Once the correct shape is obtained, appropriate additions (e.g., rearfoot posts, cut-outs, metatarsal pads) can be made to elicit the desired mechanical and/or accommodative effect.

Manufacturing technology has advanced over recent years with the emergence and increasing popularity of 3D printing. Three-D-printed foot orthoses, now commonly used by podiatrists, are similar to both traditionally pressed thermoplastic devices and milled devices. However, the main advantage presently is that they are more environmentally friendly, with no cut-off or ground-away plastic waste. As 3D technology improves, even greater potential benefits will emerge, such as being able to blend multiple materials with differing densities, to print complex geometries that can improve effect and comfort in some difficult foot cases, and perhaps save weight without any impact on the desired effect.

A common question about foot orthoses: Can I only use custom foot orthoses in neutral running shoes?

The selection of running shoes and how an individual's custom foot orthoses interact with them are important variables to consider. Foot orthoses can obviously only be used while wearing shoes. The running shoe midsole needs to provide a stable platform so that custom foot orthoses can realise their full effect. Indeed, it is the combination of features that tries to achieve the desired change in forces under the foot.

There is a common misconception that the combination of custom foot orthoses and traditional stability running shoes is too supportive and over-corrects the wearer. This is incorrect. As discussed in chapter 6, the foot-functional goal of a stability type running shoe is *not* to try and roll the feet out but to try and decrease the amount of pronation (foot rolling in). How much stability shoes can actually reduce the amount of over-pronation and do what brands claim they do is arguable, as also discussed in chapter 6.

Rest assured that if a traditional stability type running shoe is recommended for you by a podiatrist, it is perfectly acceptable to pair it with a custom foot orthosis.

For some runners, a traditional *neutral* running shoe may be more suitable, which is why the pairing of running shoes with custom foot orthoses should be assessed on a case-by-case basis, by a suitably experienced and running-shoe-knowledgeable podiatrist. If there are any signs that the combination may be adversely interfering with the runner's biomechanics, or if the combination is uncomfortable, shoe selection and foot orthosis design may need to be reconsidered. This is all part of the customisation process and needs to be dealt with by the prescribing podiatrist.

Acknowledgements

To researchers, thank you for providing us with the knowledge that allows us to provide best care and advice to our patients.

To my godmother Rosemary and her husband Jim, it has been a privilege to have you do the illustrations and pictures for this book.

To colleagues Podiatrist Tim Boyle (Managing director Sports & Spinal Podiatry), Podiatrist Justin Hogg (Owner Foot Faults Podiatry & Running Analysis Centre, Brisbane), Physiotherapist Bruno Rebello (Practice leader Sports & Spinal Physiotherapy Robina, Gold Coast), Physiotherapist Marty Cahill, and Academic/Podiatrist/ Engineer Alex Terrell. Thank you for your invaluable advice and feedback about different parts of the book.

To Physiotherapists Brad Beer and Lewis Craig (POGO physio, Gold Coast) thank you for initially inspiring me with your passion for helping runners.

To Pat Carroll, an Australian running and coaching legend, it is an absolute privilege to have had you read the book as well as provide the first comment.

To David and the team at Longueville Media thank you for nurturing "my baby" into a polished book and for your patience with me. I could not recommend your publishing services highly enough to aspiring authors.

To the Dent Global team, in particular Mike Reid and Andrew Griffiths, thank you for your encouragement as well as giving me the framework for writing this book. Starting this book would not have eventuated if not for the support of your program – The Key Person of Influence. I could not recommend this program highly enough to any small business owner.

References

ALLEN, D. J.; HEISLER, H.; MOONEY, J.; KRING, R. The Effect of Step Rate Manipulation on Foot Strike of Long Distance Runners. *Int J Sports Phys Ther*, v. 11, n. 1, pp. 54–63, Feb 2016. ISSN 2159-2896.

ALMEIDA, M. O.; DAVIS, I. S.; LOPES, A. D. What are the main running-related musculoskeletal injuries? A Systematic Review. *Sports Med*, v. 42, n. 10, pp. 891–905, Oct 2012. ISSN 1179-2035.

ALTMAN, A. R.; DAVIS, I. S. Barefoot running: biomechanics and implications for running injuries. *Curr Sports Med Rep*, v. 11, n. 5, pp. 244–50, 2012 Sep-Oct 2012. ISSN 1537-8918.

ANDERSON, L. M.; BONANNO, D. R.; HART, H. F.; BARTON, C. J. What are the Benefits and Risks Associated with Changing Foot Strike Pattern During Running? A Systematic Review and Meta-analysis of Injury, Running Economy, and Biomechanics. *Sports Medicine*, December 10 2019. ISSN 1179-2035.

BANWELL, H. A.; MACKINTOSH, S.; THEWLIS, D. Foot orthoses for adults with flexible pes planus: a systematic review. *Journal of Foot and Ankle Research*, v. 7, n. 1, p. 23, 2014. ISSN 1757-1146.

BARAVARIAN, B.; REDKAR, A. Expert insights to treating plantar plate tears. *Podiatry Today*, v. 29, n. 3, pp. 60-3, 2016.

BOELCH, S. P.; JANSEN, H.; MEFFERT, R. H.; FREY, S. P. Six Sesamoid Bones on Both Feet: Report of a Rare Case. *J Clin Diagn Res*, v. 9, n. 8, pp. RD04–5, Aug 2015. ISSN 2249-782X.

BONACCI, J.; SAUNDERS, P. U.; HICKS, A.; RANTALAINEN, T.; VICENZINO, B. G.; SPRATFORD, W. Running in a minimalist and lightweight shoe is not the same as running barefoot: a biomechanical study. *Br J Sports Med*, v. 47, n. 6, pp. 387–92, Apr 2013. ISSN 1473-0480.

BONANNO, D. R.; LANDORF, K. B.; MUNTEANU, S. E.; MURLEY, G. S.; MENZ, H. B. Effectiveness of foot orthoses and shock-absorbing insoles for the prevention of injury: a systematic review and meta-analysis. *Br J Sports Med*, v. 51, n. 2, pp. 86-96, Jan 2017. ISSN 1473-0480.

BORDONI, B.; VARACALLO, M. Anatomy, Tendons: StatPearls Publishing LLC. 2018.

BOURNE, M.; VARACALLO, M. Anatomy, Bony Pelvis and Lower Limb, Foot Fascia. In: (Ed.). *StatPearls*. Treasure Island (FL): StatPearls Publishing LLC., 2018.

BOYER, E. R.; DERRICK, T. R. Select injury-related variables are affected by stride length and foot strike style during running. *Am J Sports Med*, v. 43, n. 9, pp. 2310-17, Sep 2015. ISSN 1552-3365.

BURNS, G. T.; TAM, N. Is it the shoes? A simple proposal for regulating footwear in road running. *British Journal of Sports Medicine*, 2019. ISSN 0306-3674.

BURNS, J.; LANDORF, K. B.; RYAN, M. M.; CROSBIE, J.; OUVRIER, R. A. Interventions for the prevention and treatment of pes cavus. *Cochrane Database of Systematic Reviews*, n. 4, 2007. ISSN 1465-1858.

CHAN, Z. Y. S.; AU, I. P. H.; LAU, F. O. Y.; CHING, E. C. K.; ZHANG, J. H.; CHEUNG, R. T. H. Does maximalist footwear lower impact loading during level ground and downhill running? *Eur J Sport Sci*, v. 18, n. 8, pp. 1083-9, Sep 2018. ISSN 1536-7290.

CHEN, D. W.; LI, B.; AUBEELUCK, A.; YANG, Y. F.; HUANG, Y. G.; ZHOU, J. Q.; YU, G. R. Anatomy and biomechanical properties of the plantar aponeurosis: a cadaveric study. *PLoS ONE*, v. 9, n. 1, pp. 843-47, 2014. ISSN 1932-6203.

CHEUNG, R. T.; NGAI, S. P. Effects of footwear on running economy in distance runners: A meta-analytical review. *J Sci Med Sport*, v. 19, n. 3, pp. 260-6, Mar 2016. ISSN 1878-1861.

COOK, S. D.; KESTER, M. A.; BRUNET, M. E. Shock absorption characteristics of running shoes. *Am J Sports Med*, v. 13, n. 4, pp. 248-53, 1985 Jul-Aug 1985. ISSN 0363-5465.

DA SILVA AZEVEDO, A. P.; MEZENCIO, B.; VALVASSORI, R.; MOCHIZUKI, L.; AMADIO, A. C.; SERRAO, J. C. Does 'transition shoe' promote an intermediate biomechanical condition compared to running in conventional shoe and in reduced protection condition? *Gait Posture*, v. 46, pp. 142-6, May 2016. ISSN 1879-2219.

DAOUD, A. I.; GEISSLER, G. J.; WANG, F.; SARETSKY, J.; DAOUD, Y. A.; LIEBERMAN, D. E. Foot strike and injury rates in endurance runners: a retrospective study. *Med Sci Sports Exerc*, v. 44, n. 7, pp. 1325-34, Jul 2012. ISSN 1530-0315.

DAVIS, I. S.; RICE, H. M.; WEARING, S. C. Why forefoot striking in minimal shoes might positively change the course of running injuries. *Journal of Sport and Health Science*, v. 6, n. 2, pp. 154-61, 2017. ISSN 2095-2546.

DELAND, J. T.; LEE, K. T.; SOBEL, M.; DICARLO, E. F. Anatomy of the plantar plate and its attachments in the lesser metatarsal phalangeal joint. *Foot Ankle Int*, v. 16, n. 8, pp. 480-6, Aug 1995. ISSN 1071-1007.

DORAL, M. N.; ALAM, M.; BOZKURT, M.; TURHAN, E.; ATAY, O. A.; DONMEZ, G.; MAFFULLI, N. Functional anatomy of the Achilles tendon. *Knee Surg Sports Traumatol Arthrosc*, v. 18, n. 5, pp. 638-43, May 2010. ISSN 1433-7347.

DORLAND, W. A. N. *Dorland's Illustrated Medical Dictionary*: Saunders 2003. ISBN 0-7216-0146-4

ESCULIER, J. F.; DUBOIS, B.; DIONNE, C. E.; LEBLOND, J.; ROY, J. S. A consensus definition and rating scale for minimalist shoes. *J Foot Ankle Res*, v. 8, p. 42, 2015. ISSN 1757-1146.

FIELDS, K. B. et al. Prevention of running injuries. *Curr Sports Med Rep*, v. 9, n. 3, pp. 176-82, 2010 May-Jun 2010. ISSN 1537-8918.

FREDERICK, E. C.; DANIELS, J. R.; HAYES, J. W. The effect of shoe weight on the aerobic demands of running. *Current Topics in Sports Medicine*, pp. 616-25, 1984.

FULLER, J. T.; BELLENGER, C.; THEWLIS, D.; TSIROS, M. D.; BUCKLEY, J. D. The Effect of Footwear on Running Performance and Running Economy in Distance Runners. *Sports Medicine*, Cham, v. 45, n. 3, pp. 411-22, 2015. ISSN 0112-1642.

FULLER, J. T.; THEWLIS, D.; BUCKLEY, J. D.; BROWN, N. A.; HAMILL, J.; TSIROS, M. D. Body Mass and Weekly Training Distance Influence the Pain and Injuries Experienced by Runners Using Minimalist Shoes: A Randomized Controlled Trial. *Am J Sports Med*, v. 45, n. 5, pp. 1162-70, Apr 2017. ISSN 1552-3365.

FULLER, J. T.; THEWLIS, D.; TSIROS, M. D.; BROWN, N. A. T.; BUCKLEY, J. D. Effects of a minimalist shoe on running economy and 5-km running performance. *Journal of Sports Sciences*, v. 34, n. 18, pp. 1740-5, 2016. ISSN 0264-0414.

GALLANT, J. L.; PIERRYNOWSKI, M. R. A theoretical perspective on running-related injuries. *J Am Podiatr Med Assoc*, v. 104, n. 2, pp. 211-20, Mar 2014. ISSN 1930-8264.

GALLO, R. A.; PLAKKE, M.; SILVIS, M. L. Common leg injuries of long-distance runners: anatomical and biomechanical approach. *Sports Health*, v. 4, n. 6, pp. 485-95, Nov 2012. ISSN 1941-0921.

GERRARD, J. M.; BONANNO, D. R. Increasing preferred step rate during running reduces plantar pressures. *Scand J Med Sci Sports*, v. 28, n. 1, pp. 144-51, Jan 2018. ISSN 1600-0838.

GLENN, N. O.; HENRY, C. A. How muscle contraction strengthens tendons. *Elife*, v. 8, pp. 1-3, Jan 2019. ISSN 2050-084X.

GRIER, T.; CANHAM-CHERVAK, M.; BUSHMAN, T.; ANDERSON, M.; NORTH, W.; JONES, B. H. Minimalist Running Shoes and Injury Risk Among United States Army Soldiers. *Am J Sports Med*, v. 44, n. 6, pp. 1439-46, Jun 2016. ISSN 1552-3365.

HADJIDAKIS, D. J.; ANDROULAKIS, I. I. Bone remodeling. *Ann N Y Acad Sci*, v. 1092, pp. 385-96, Dec 2006. ISSN 0077-8923.

HALL, J. P.; BARTON, C.; JONES, P. R.; MORRISSEY, D. The biomechanical differences between barefoot and shod distance running: a systematic review and preliminary meta-analysis. *Sports Med*, v. 43, n. 12, pp. 1335-53, Dec 2013. ISSN 1179-2035.

HASEGAWA, H.; YAMAUCHI, T.; KRAEMER, W. J. Foot strike patterns of runners at the 15-km point during an elite-level half marathon. *J Strength Cond Res*, v. 21, n. 3, pp. 888-93, Aug 2007. ISSN 1064-8011.

HAUSER, R. A.; DOLAN, E. E.; PHILLIPS, H. J.; NEWLIN, A.C.; MOORE, R.E.; WOLDIN, B.A. Ligament Injury and Healing: A Review of Current Clinical Diagnostics and Therapeutics. *The Open Rehabilitation Journal*, v. 6, pp. 1-20, 2013.

HEIDERSCHEIT, B. C.; CHUMANOV, E. S.; MICHALSKI, M. P.; WILLE, C. M.; RYAN, M. B. Effects of step rate manipulation on joint mechanics during running. *Med Sci Sports Exerc*, v. 43, n. 2, pp. 296-302, Feb 2011. ISSN 1530-0315.

HICKS, J. H. The mechanics of the foot. II. The plantar aponeurosis and the arch. *Journal of Anatomy*, v. 88, n. 1, p. 25, 1954. ISSN 0021-8782.

HOLLOSZY, J. O. Adaptation of skeletal muscle to endurance exercise. *Med Sci Sports*, v. 7, n. 3, pp. 155-64, 1975. ISSN 0025-7990.

HOOGKAMER, W.; KIPP, S.; FRANK, J. H.; FARINA, E. M.; LUO, G.; KRAM, R. A Comparison of the Energetic Cost of Running in Marathon Racing Shoes. *Sports Med*, v. 48, n. 4, pp. 1009-19, April 2018. ISSN 1179-2035.

HOSSAIN, M.; ALEXANDER, P.; BURLS, A.; JOBANPUTRA, P. Foot orthoses for patellofemoral pain in adults. *Cochrane Bone, Joint and Muscle Trauma Group*, Chichester, UK, n. 1, 2011. ISSN 1465-1858.

HRELJAC, A. Impact and overuse injuries in runners. *Med Sci Sports Exerc*, v. 36, n. 5, pp. 845–9, May 2004. ISSN 0195-9131.

HRELJAC, A.; MARSHALL, R. N.; HUME, P. A. Evaluation of lower extremity overuse injury potential in runners. *Med Sci Sports Exerc*, v. 32, n. 9, pp. 1635–41, Sep 2000. ISSN 0195-9131.

HUFFER, D.; HING, W.; NEWTON, R.; CLAIR, M. Strength training for plantar fasciitis and the intrinsic foot musculature: A systematic review. *Phys Ther Sport*, v. 24, pp. 44–52, Mar 2017. ISSN 1873-1600.

IRWIN, T. A. Current concepts review: insertional achilles tendinopathy. *Foot Ankle Int*, v. 31, n. 10, pp. 933–9, Oct 2010. ISSN 1071-1007.

JEFFREY, A. R. A comprehensive guide to reviving the sick sesamoid. *Podiatry Today*, v. 29, n. 4, pp. 68–71, 2016.

JENKINS, D. W.; CAUTHON, D. J. Barefoot running claims and controversies: a review of the literature. *J Am Podiatr Med Assoc*, v. 101, n. 3, pp. 231–46, May-Jun 2011. ISSN 1930-8264.

JUNG, D. Y.; KOH, E. K.; KWON, O. Y. Effect of foot orthoses and short-foot exercise on the cross-sectional area of the abductor hallucis muscle in subjects with pes planus: a randomized controlled trial. *Journal of Back and Musculoskeletal Rehabilitation*, v. 24, n. 4, p. 225, 2011. ISSN 1053-8127.

KANNUS, P. Structure of the tendon connective tissue. *Scand J Med Sci Sports*, v. 10, n. 6, pp. 312–20, Dec 2000. ISSN 0905-7188.

KARANDIKAR, N.; VARGAS, O. O. Kinetic chains: a review of the concept and its clinical applications. *Pm&R*, v. 3, n. 8, pp. 739–45, Aug 2011. ISSN 1934-1482.

KASMER, M. E.; LIU, X. C.; ROBERTS, K. G.; VALADAO, J. M. Foot-strike pattern and performance in a marathon. *Int J Sports Physiol Perform*, v. 8, n. 3, pp. 286–92, May 2013. ISSN 1555-0265.

KELLY, L. A.; CRESSWELL, A. G.; RACINAIS, S; WHITELEY, R.; LICHTWARK, G. Intrinsic foot muscles have the capacity to control deformation of the longitudinal arch. *Journal of the Royal Society, Interface*, v. 11, n. 93, 20131188, pp. 1-9, 2014. ISSN 1742-5689.

KIEL J.; KAISER, K. *Stress Reaction and Fractures. In: StatPearls [Internet]*. : Treasure Island (FL): StatPearls Publishing; 2018 Jan-. [Updated 2018 Oct 27].

KIRBY, K. Understanding The Biomechanics of Plantar Plate Injuries. *Podiatry Today*, v. 30, n. 4, pp. 30–9, 2017.

KONG, P. W.; CANDELARIA, N. G.; SMITH, D. R. Running in new and worn shoes: a comparison of three types of cushioning footwear. *British Journal of Sports Medicine*, v. 43, n. 10, pp. 745, 2009. ISSN 0306-3674.

KULMALA, J. P.; KISONEN, J.; NURMINEN, J.; AVELA, J. Running in highly cushioned shoes increases leg stiffness and amplifies impact loading. *Sci Rep*, v. 8, n. 1, p. 17496, Nov 2018. ISSN 2045-2322.

LANDORF, K. B. Plantar heel pain and plantar fasciitis. *BMJ Clin Evid*, v. 2015, Nov 2015. ISSN 1752-8526.

LARSON, P.; HIGGINS, E.; KAMINSKI, J.; DECKER, T.; PREBLE, J.; LYONS, D.; McINTYRE, K.; NORMILE, A. Foot strike patterns of recreational and sub-elite runners in a long-distance road race. *J Sports Sci*, v. 29, n. 15, pp. 1665–73, Dec 2011. ISSN 1466-447X.

LATEY, P. J.; BURNS, J.; HILLER, C. E.; NIGHTINGALE, E. J. Relationship between foot pain, muscle strength and size: a systematic review. *Physiotherapy*, v. 103, n. 1, pp. 13–20, Mar 2017. ISSN 1873-1465.

LI, H. Y.; HUA, Y. H. Achilles Tendinopathy: Current Concepts about the Basic Science and Clinical Treatments. *Biomed Res Int*, v. 2016, pp. 1–10, 2016. ISSN 2314-6141.

LIEBERMAN, D. E. Human evolution: Those feet in ancient times. *Nature*, v. 483, n. 7391, pp. 550–1, Mar 2012. ISSN 1476-4687.

LIEBERMAN, D. E.; VENKADESAN, M.; WERBEL, W. A.; DAOUD, A. I.; D'ANDREA, S.; DAVIS, I. S.; MANG'ENI, R. O.; PITSILADIS, Y. Foot strike patterns and collision forces in habitually barefoot versus shod runners. *Nature*, v. 463, n. 7280, pp. 531–5, Jan 2010. ISSN 1476-4687.

LORIMER, D. L., & NEALE, D. *Neale's Disorders of the Foot: Diagnosis and Management*. Edinburgh: Churchill Livingstone, 2003. Print. ISBN-13: 978-0443064418

LUCAS, R.; CORNWALL, M. Influence of foot posture on the functioning of the windlass mechanism. *Foot (Edinb)*, v. 30, pp. 38–42, Mar 2017. ISSN 1532-2963.

LYGHT, M.; NOCKERTS, M.; KERNOZEK, T. W.; RAGAN, R. Effects of Foot Strike and Step Frequency on Achilles Tendon Stress During Running. *J Appl Biomech*, v. 32, n. 4, pp. 365–72, Aug 2016. ISSN 1543-2688.

MALISOUX, L.; CHAMBON, N.; URHAUSEN, A.; THEISEN, D. Influence of the Heel-to-Toe Drop of Standard Cushioned Running Shoes on Injury Risk in Leisure-Time Runners: A Randomized Controlled Trial With 6-Month Follow-up. *Am J Sports Med*, v. 44, n. 11, pp. 2933–40, Nov 2016. ISSN 1552-3365.

MALISOUX, L.; RAMESH, J.; MANN, R.; SEIL, R.; URHAUSEN, A.; THEISEN, D. Can parallel use of different running shoes decrease running-related injury risk? *Scandinavian Journal of Medicine & Science in Sports*, v. 25, n. 1, pp. 110–15, 2015. ISSN 0905-7188.

MARIEB, E. N.; HOEHN, K. *Human Anatomy & Physiology*. 8th. San Francisco, CA, USA: Pearson Benjamin Cummings, 2010. ISBN: 978-0-321-60261-9

MCDOUGALL, C. Born to Run: A hidden tribe, superathletes, and the greatest race the world has never seen. New York.: Knopf, 2009. ISBN 13 9781861978776.

MCKEON, P. O.; HERTEL, J.; BRAMBLE, D.; DAVIS, I. The foot core system: a new paradigm for understanding intrinsic foot muscle function. *British Journal of Sports Medicine*, v. 49, n. 5, p. 290, 2015. ISSN 0306-3674.

MCPOIL THOMAS, G.; CORNWALL MARK, W. Relationship between static foot posture and foot mobility. *Journal of Foot and Ankle Research*, v. 4, n. 1, p. 4, 2011. ISSN 1757-1146.

MCSWEENEY, S. First Metatarsophalangeal joint Osteoarthritis - A clinical review. *Journal of Novel Physiotherapies*, v. 6, p. 293, 2016.

MENZ, H. B. Foot orthoses: how much customisation is necessary? *Journal of Foot and Ankle Research*, v. 2, n. 1, p. 23, 2009. ISSN 1757-1146.

MILLER, E. E.; WHITCOME, K. K.; LIEBERMAN, D. E.; NORTON, H. L.; DYER, R. E. The effect of minimal shoes on arch structure and intrinsic foot muscle strength. *Journal of Sport and Health Science*, v. 3, n. 2, pp. 74–85, 2014. ISSN 2095-2546.

MONTEAGUDO, M.; DE ALBORNOZ, P. M.; GUTIERREZ, B.; TABUENCA, J.; ALVAREZ, I. Plantar fasciopathy: A current concepts review. *EFORT Open Rev*, v. 3, n. 8, pp. 485–93, Aug 2018. ISSN 2058-5241 (Print).

MURLEY, G. S.; LANDORF, K. B.; MENZ, H. B. Do foot orthoses change lower limb muscle activity in flat-arched feet towards a pattern observed in normal-arched feet? *Clinical Biomechanics*, v. 25, n. 7, pp. 728–36, 2010. ISSN 0268-0033.

MURLEY, G. S.; LANDORF, K. B.; MENZ, H. B.; BIRD, A. R. Effect of foot posture, foot orthoses and footwear on lower limb muscle activity during walking and running: A systematic review. *Gait & Posture*, v. 29, n. 2, pp. 172–87, 2009. ISSN 0966-6362.

MURPHY, K.; CURRY, E. J.; MATZKIN, E. G. Barefoot Running: Does It Prevent Injuries? *Sports Med*, v. 43, n. 11, pp. 1131–8, Nov 2013. ISSN 1179-2035.

MYBURGH, K. H.; WESTON, A. R. The human endurance athlete: heterogeneity and adaptability of selected exercise and skeletal muscle characteristics. *South African Journal of Zoology*, v. 33, n. 2, pp. 129–40, 1998.

NAPIER, C.; WILLY, R. W. Logical fallacies in the running shoe debate: let the evidence guide prescription. *British Journal of Sports Medicine*, v. 52, n. 24, pp. 1552-1553, 2018. ISSN 0306-3674.

NEAL, B. S.; GRIFFITHS, I. B.; DOWLING, G. J.; MURLEY, G. S.; MUNTEANU, S. E.; FRANETTOVICH SMITH, M. M.; COLLINS, N. J.; BARTON, C. J. Foot posture as a risk factor for lower limb overuse injury: A systematic review and meta-analysis. *Journal of Foot and Ankle Research*, v. 7, n. 1, 2014. ISSN 1757-1146.

NICHOLAS, B. H.; IAN, J. W.; DANIEL, E. L. Foot strength and stiffness are related to footwear use in a comparison of minimally- vs. conventionally-shod populations. *Scientific Reports*, v. 8, n. 1, pp. 1–12, 2018. ISSN 2045-2322.

NIELSON, R. O.; BUIST, I.; PARNER, E. T.; NOHR, E. A.; SORENSEN, H.; LIND, M.; RASMUSSEN, S. Foot pronation is not associated with increased injury risk in novice runners wearing a neutral shoe: a 1-year prospective cohort study. *Br J Sports Med*, v. 48, n. 6, pp. 440–7, Mar 2014. ISSN 1473-0480.

NIGG, B. M.; BALTICH, J.; HOERZER, S.; ENDERS, H. Running shoes and running injuries: mythbusting and a proposal for two new paradigms: 'preferred movement path' and 'comfort filter'. *Br J Sports Med*, v. 49, n. 20, pp. 1290–4, Oct 2015. ISSN 1473-0480.

NIGG, B. M.; VIENNEAU, J.; SMITH, A. C.; TRUDEAU, M. B.; MOHR, M.; NIGG, S. R. The Preferred Movement Path Paradigm: Influence of Running Shoes on Joint Movement. *Med Sci Sports Exerc*, v. 49, n. 8, pp. 1641–8, Aug 2017. ISSN 1530-0315.

NOAKES, T. D. *Lore of Running*. 4th ed. Oxford University Press, Southern Africa, 2001. ISBN: 9780873229593

NOSE-OGURA, S.; HARADA, M.; HIRAIKE, O.; OSUGA, Y.; FUJII, T. Management of the female athlete triad. *J Obstet Gynaecol Res*, Apr 2018. ISSN 1447-0756.

NOVACHECK, T. F. The biomechanics of running. *Gait Posture*, v. 7, n. 1, pp. 77–95, Jan 1998. ISSN 1879-2219.

PEKALA, P. A.; HENRY, B. M.; PEKALA, J. R.; PISKA, K.; TOMASZEWSKI, K. A. The Achilles tendon and the retrocalcaneal bursa: An anatomical and radiological study. *Bone Joint Res*, v. 6, n. 7, pp. 446-51, Jul 2017. ISSN 2046-3758.

PERKINS, K. P.; HANNEY, W. J.; ROTHSCHILD, C. E. The risks and benefits of running barefoot or in minimalist shoes: a systematic review. *Sports Health*, v. 6, n. 6, pp. 475-80, Nov 2014. ISSN 1941-7381.

PERL, D. P.; DAOUD, A. I.; LIEBERMAN, D. E. Effects of footwear and strike type on running economy. *Med Sci Sports Exerc*, v. 44, n. 7, pp. 1335-43, Jul 2012. ISSN 1530-0315.

PETRAGLIA, F.; RAMAZZINA, I.; COSTANTINO, C. Plantar fasciitis in athletes: diagnostic and treatment strategies. A systematic review. *Muscles Ligaments Tendons J*, v. 7, n. 1, pp. 107-118, 2017 Jan-Mar 2017. ISSN 2240-4554.

RALPHS, J. R.; BENJAMIN, M. The joint capsule: structure, composition, ageing and disease. *J Anat*, v. 184 (Pt 3), pp. 503-9, Jun 1994. ISSN 0021-8782.

RETHNAM, U.; MAKWANA, N. Are old running shoes detrimental to your feet? A pedobarographic study. *BMC Research Notes*, London, v. 4, n. 1, p. 307, 2011. ISSN 1756-0500.

RICHARDS, C. E.; MAGIN, P. J.; CALLISTER, R. Is your prescription of distance running shoes evidence-based? *Br J Sports Med*, v. 43, n. 3, pp. 159-62, Mar 2009. ISSN 1473-0480.

ROBBINS, S. E.; HANNA, A. M. Running-related injury prevention through barefoot adaptations. *Medicine and Science in Sports and Exercise*, v. 19, n. 2, pp. 148-56, 1987. ISSN 0195-9131.

ROCHE, A. J.; CALDER, J. D. Achilles tendinopathy: A review of the current concepts of treatment. *Bone Joint J*, v. 95-B, n. 10, pp. 1299-307, Oct 2013. ISSN 2049-4408.

RODOLA, C. G.; CAPPELLO, F.; MARCIANO, V.; FRANCAVILLA, C.; MONTALLBANO, A.; FARINA LIPARI, E.; PALMA, A. The synovial joints of the human foot. *Ital J Anat Embryol*, v. 112, n. 2, pp. 61-80, Apr-Jun 2007. ISSN 1122-6714 (Print). 1122-6714.

SARAGIOTTO, B. T.; YAMATO, T. P.; HESPANHOL JUNIOR, L. C.; RAINBOW, M. J.; DAVIS, I. S.; LOPES, A. D. What are the main risk factors for running-related injuries? *Sports Med*, v. 44, n. 8, pp. 1153-63, Aug 2014. ISSN 1179-2035.

SCHEPSIS, A. A.; JONES, H.; HAAS, A. L. Achilles tendon disorders in athletes. *Am J Sports Med*, v. 30, n. 2, pp. 287-305, 2002 Mar-Apr 2002. ISSN 0363-5465.

SIMONEAU, J. A.; BOUCHARD, C. Genetic determinism of fiber type proportion in human skeletal muscle. *FASEB J*, v. 9, n. 11, pp. 1091-5, Aug 1995. ISSN 0892-6638.

SOBHANI, S.; VAN DEN HEUVEL, E. R.; DEKKER, R.; POSTEMA, K.; KLUITENBERG, B.; BREDEWEG, S. W.; HIJMANS, J. M. Biomechanics of running with rocker shoes. *J Sci Med Sport*, v. 20, n. 1, pp. 38-44, Jan 2017. ISSN 1878-1861.

SOBHANI, S.; VAN DEN HEUVEL, E.; BREDEWEG, S.; KLUITENBERG, B.; POSTEMA, K.; HIJMANS, J. M.; DEKKER, R. Effect of rocker shoes on plantar pressure pattern in healthy female runners. *Gait Posture*, v. 39, n. 3, pp. 920-5, Mar 2014. ISSN 1879-2219.

SOBHANI, S.; ZWERVER, J.; VAN DEN HEUVEL, E.; POSTEMA, K., DEKKER, R.; HIJMANS, J. M. Rocker shoes reduce Achilles tendon load in running and walking in patients with chronic Achilles tendinopathy. *J Sci Med Sport*, v. 18, n. 2, pp. 133-8, Mar 2015. ISSN 1878-1861.

SOPHIA FOX, A. J.; BEDI, A.; RODEO, S. A. The basic science of articular cartilage: structure, composition, and function. *Sports Health*, v. 1, n. 6, pp. 461-8, Nov 2009. ISSN 1941-7381.

SQUADRONE, R.; GALLOZZI, C. Biomechanical and physiological comparison of barefoot and two shod conditions in experienced barefoot runners. *J Sports Med Phys Fitness*, v. 49, n. 1, pp. 6-13, Mar 2009. ISSN 0022-4707.

STECCO, C.; MACCHI, V.; PORZIONATO, A.; DUPARC, F.; DE CARO, R. The fascia: the forgotten structure. *Ital J Anat Embryol*, v. 116, n. 3, pp. 127-38, 2011. ISSN 1122-6714.

SULLIVAN, J.; BURNS, J.; ADAMS, R.; PAPPAS, E.; CROSBIE, J. Musculoskeletal and activity-related factors associated with plantar heel pain. *Foot Ankle Int*, v. 36, n. 1, pp. 37-45, Jan 2015. ISSN 1944-7876.

TALBOT, J.; MAVES, L. Skeletal muscle fiber type: using insights from muscle developmental biology to dissect targets for susceptibility and resistance to muscle disease. *Wiley Interdiscip Rev Dev Biol*, v. 5, n. 4, pp. 518-34, 07 2016. ISSN 1759-7692.

TAM, N.; ASTEPHEN WILSON, J. L.; NOAKES, T. D.; TUCKER, R. Barefoot running: an evaluation of current hypothesis, future research and clinical applications. *Br J Sports Med*, v. 48, n. 5, pp. 349-55, Mar 2014. ISSN 1473-0480.

TUNG, K. D.; FRANZ, J. R.; KRAM, R. A test of the metabolic cost of cushioning hypothesis during unshod and shod running. *Medicine and Science in Sports and Exercise*, v. 46, n. 2, p. 324, 2014. ISSN 0195-9131.

VAN DER WORP, H.; VRIELINK, J. W.; BREDEWEG, S. W. Do runners who suffer injuries have higher vertical ground reaction forces than those who remain injury-free? A systematic review and meta-analysis. *Br J Sports Med*, v. 50, n. 8, pp. 450-7, Apr 2016. ISSN 1473-0480.

VAN DER WORP, M. P.; TEN HAAF, D. S.; VAN CINGEL, R.; DE WIJER, A.; NIJHUIS-VAN DER SANDEN, M. W.; STAAL, J. B. Injuries in runners: a systematic review on risk factors and sex differences. *PLoS ONE*, 10(2): 0114937, 2015. ISSN 1932-6203.

VAN GENT, R. N.; SIEM, D.; VAN MIDDELKOOP, M.; VAN OS, A. G.; BIERMA-ZEINSTRA, S. M. A.; KOES, B. W. Incidence and determinants of lower extremity running injuries in long distance runners: a systematic review. In: (Ed.). *Br J Sports Med*, v. 41, 2007. pp. 469-80. ISBN 0306-3674 (Print).

WAGER, J. C.; CHALLIS, J. H. Elastic energy within the human plantar aponeurosis contributes to arch shortening during the push-off phase of running. *Journal of Biomechanics*, v. 49, n. 5, pp. 704-9, 2016. ISSN 0021-9290.

WANG, L.; XIAN L. J.; HONG, Y.; HE ZHOU, J. Changes in heel cushioning characteristics of running shoes with running mileage. *Footwear Science*, v. 2, n. 3, pp. 141-7, 2010. ISSN 1942-4280.

WARR, B. J.; FELLIN, R. E.; SAUER, S. G.; GOSS, D. L.; FRYKMAN, P. N.; SEAY, J. F. Characterization of Foot-Strike Patterns: Lack of an Association with

Injuries or Performance in Soldiers. *Mil Med*, v. 180, n. 7, pp. 830–4, Jul 2015. ISSN 1930-613X.

WEN, D. Y. Risk factors for overuse injuries in runners. *Curr Sports Med Rep*, v. 6, n. 5, pp. 307–13, Oct 2007. ISSN 1537-8918.

WERD, M. B., KNIGHT, E. L., LANGER, P. R. *Athletic Footwear & Orthoses in Sports Medicine. Evolution of Athletic Footwear.* SUBOTNICK, S. I.: Springer International Publishing 2017.

WHITTAKER, G. A.; MUNTEANU, S. E.; MENZ, H. B.; TAN, J. M.; RABUSIN, C. L.; LANDORF, K. B. Foot orthoses for plantar heel pain: a systematic review and meta-analysis. *Br J Sports Med*, v. 52, n. 5, pp. 322–8, Mar 2018. ISSN 1473-0480.

WILLIAMS III, D. S.; MCCLAY, I. S.; HAMILL, J. Arch structure and injury patterns in runners. *Clinical Biomechanics*, v. 16, n. 4, pp. 341–7, 2001. ISSN 0268-0033.

WOROBETS, J; WANNOP, J. W.; TOMARAS, E.; STEFANYSHYN, D. Softer and more resilient running shoe cushioning properties enhance running economy. *Footwear Science*, v. 6, n. 3, pp. 147–53, 2014. ISSN 1942-4280.

www.hokaoneone.com/brand-origins.html. Accessed: 6th July 2019.

www.triathlete.com/2018/10/gear-tech/kona-2018-running-shoe-count-hoka-reigns-again_336635. Kona 2018 Running Shoe Count: Hoka Reigns Again. 2018. Accessed: 6th July 2019.

YAMATO, T. P.; SARAGIOTTO, B. T.; LOPES, A. D. A consensus definition of running-related injury in recreational runners: a modified Delphi approach. *J Orthop Sports Phys Ther*, v. 45, n. 5, pp. 375–80, May 2015. ISSN 1938-1344.

ZIMMERMANN, W. O.; BAKKER, E. W. P. Reducing vertical ground reaction forces: The relative importance of three gait retraining cues. *Clinical Biomechanics*, v. 69, pp. 16-20, 2019. ISSN 0268-0033.

Endnotes

1 FIELDS, K. B. et al., Prevention of running injuries. *Curr Sports Med Rep*, v. 9, n. 3, pp. 176–82, 2010 May–Jun 2010. ISSN 1537-8918.

2 GALLANT, J. L.; PIERRYNOWSKI, M. R., A theoretical perspective on running-related injuries. *J Am Podiatr Med Assoc*, v. 104, n. 2, pp. 211–20, Mar 2014. ISSN 1930-8264. See also HRELJAC, A. Impact and overuse injuries in runners. *Med Sci Sports Exerc*, v. 36, n. 5, pp. 845–9, May 2004. ISSN 0195-9131.

3 GALLANT, A theoretical perspective on running-related injuries. *J Am Podiatr Med Assoc*, pp. 211–20; see also HRELJAC, Impact and overuse injuries in runners, pp. 845–9.

4 WEN, D. Y., Risk factors for overuse injuries in runners. *Curr Sports Med Rep*, v. 6, n. 5, pp. 307–13, Oct 2007. ISSN 1537-8918. See also HRELJAC, A.; MARSHALL, R. N.; HUME, P. A., Evaluation of lower extremity overuse injury potential in runners. *Med Sci Sports Exerc*, v. 32, n. 9, pp. 1635–41, Sep 2000. ISSN 0195-9131.

5 HRELJAC, A.; MARSHALL, R. N.; HUME, P. A., Evaluation of lower extremity overuse injury potential in runners. *Med Sci Sports Exerc*, v. 32, n. 9, pp. 1635–41, Sep 2000. ISSN 0195-9131. See also VAN GENT, R. N.; SIEM, D.; VAN MIDDELKOOP, M.; VAN OS, A. G.; BIERMA-ZEINSTRA, S. M. A.; KOES, B. W., Incidence and determinants of lower extremity running injuries in long distance runners: a systematic review. In: (Ed.). *Br J Sports Med*, v. 41, 2007. pp. 469–80. ISBN 0306-3674 (Print). See also VAN DER WORP, M. P.; TEN HAAF, D. S.; VAN CINGEL, R.; DE WIJER, A.; NIJHUIS-VAN DER SANDEN, M. W.; STAAL, J. B. Injuries in runners: a systematic review on risk factors and sex differences. *PLoS ONE*, v. 10, n. 2, p. e0114937, 2015. ISSN 1932-6203. See also SARAGIOTTO, B. T.; YAMATO, T. P.; HESPANHOL JUNIOR, L. C.; RAINBOW, M. J.; DAVIS, I. S.; LOPES, A. D. What are the main risk factors for running-related injuries? *Sports Med*, v. 44, n. 8, pp. 1153–63, Aug 2014. ISSN 1179-2035.

6 VAN GENT, R. N.; SIEM, D.; VAN MIDDELKOOP, M.; VAN OS, A. G.; BIERMA-ZEINSTRA, S. M. A.; KOES, B. W., Incidence and determinants of lower extremity running injuries in long distance runners: a systematic review. In: (Ed.). *Br J Sports Med*, v. 41, 2007. pp. 469–80. ISBN 0306-3674 (Print). See also VAN DER WORP, M. P.; TEN HAAF, D. S.; VAN CINGEL, R.; DE WIJER, A.; NIJHUIS-VAN DER SANDEN, M. W.; STAAL, J. B. Injuries in runners: a systematic review on risk factors and sex differences. *PLoS ONE*, v. 10, n. 2, p. e0114937, 2015. ISSN 1932-6203.

7   VAN GENT, R. N.; SIEM, D.; VAN MIDDELKOOP, M.; VAN OS, A. G.;
     BIERMA-ZEINSTRA, S. M. A.; KOES, B. W., Incidence and determinants of
     lower extremity running injuries in long distance runners: a systematic review.
     In: (Ed.). *Br J Sports Med*, v. 41, 2007. pp. 469–80. ISBN 0306-3674 (Print).
     See also VAN DER WORP, M. P.; TEN HAAF, D. S.; VAN CINGEL, R.; DE
     WIJER, A.; NIJHUIS-VAN DER SANDEN, M. W.; STAAL, J. B. Injuries in
     runners: a systematic review on risk factors and sex differences. *PLoS ONE*, v.
     10, n. 2, p. e0114937, 2015. ISSN 1932-6203. See also VAN DER WORP, H.;
     VRIELINK, J. W.; BREDEWEG, S. W., Do runners who suffer injuries have
     higher vertical ground reaction forces than those who remain injury-free? A
     systematic review and meta-analysis. *Br J Sports Med*, v. 50, n. 8, po. 450–7,
     Apr 2016. ISSN 1473-0480.
8   LORIMER, D. L., & NEALE, D., *Neale's Disorders of the Foot: Diagnosis and
     Management*. Edinburgh: Churchill Livingstone, 2003. Print. ISBN-13: 978-
     0443064418.
9   LIEBERMAN, D. E., Human evolution: Those feet in ancient times. *Nature*, v.
     483, n. 7391, pp. 550–1, Mar 2012. ISSN 1476-4687.
10   MCKEON, P.O.; HERTEL, J.; BRAMBLE, D.; DAVIS, I., The foot core
     system: a new paradigm for understanding intrinsic foot muscle function.
     British Journal of Sports Medicine, v. 49, n. 5, p. 290, 2015. ISSN 0306-
     3674. See also WAGER, J. C.; CHALLIS, J. H., Elastic energy within the
     human plantar aponeurosis contributes to arch shortening during the push-
     off phase of running. *Journal of Biomechanics*, v. 49, n. 5, pp. 704–9, 2016.
     ISSN 0021-9290.
11   DA-WEI, Chen; BING, Li; ASHWIN, AUBEELUCK; YUN-FENG, YANG;
     YI-GANG, HUANG; JIA-QIAN, ZHOU; GUANG-RONG, YU. Anatomy and
     biomechanical properties of the plantar aponeurosis: a cadaveric study. *PLoS
     ONE*, v. 9, n. 1, p. e84347, 2014. ISSN 1932-6203.
12   WAGER, Elastic energy within the human plantar aponeurosis contributes to
     arch shortening during the push-off phase of running. *Journal of Biomechanics*.
13   HICKS, J. H., The mechanics of the foot. II. The plantar aponeurosis and the
     arch. *Journal of anatomy*, v. 88, n. 1, p. 25, 1954. ISSN 0021-8782.
14   LORIMER, *Neale's Disorders of the Foot: Diagnosis and Management*.
15   WILLIAMS III, D. S.; MCCLAY, I. S.; HAMILL, J., Arch structure and injury
     patterns in runners. *Clinical Biomechanics*, v. 16, n. 4, pp. 341–7, 2001.
     ISSN 0268-0033.
16   LORIMER, *Neale's Disorders of the Foot: Diagnosis and Management*.
17   WILLIAMS III, Arch structure and injury patterns in runners.
18   LORIMER, *Neale's Disorders of the Foot: Diagnosis and Management*.
19   BURNS, J.; LANDORF, K. B.; RYAN, M. M.; CROSBIE, J.; OUVRIER, R.
     A., Interventions for the prevention and treatment of pes cavus. *Cochrane
     Database of Systematic Reviews*, n. 4, 2007. ISSN 1465-1858.
20   BANWELL, H. A.; MACKINTOSH, S.; THEWLIS, D., Foot orthoses for adults
     with flexible pes planus: a systematic review. *Journal of foot and ankle research*,
     v. 7, n. 1, p. 23, 2014. ISSN 1757-1146. See also NEAL, B. S.; GRIFFITHS, I.
     B.; DOWLING, G. J.; MURLEY, G. S.; MUNTEANU, S. E.; FRANETTOVICH
     SMITH, M. M.; COLLINS, N. J.; BARTON, C. J., Foot posture as a risk factor

for lower limb overuse injury: A systematic review and meta-analysis. *Journal of Foot and Ankle Research,* v. 7, n. 1, 2014. ISSN 1757-1146.

21 NEAL, Foot posture as a risk factor for lower limb overuse injury: A systematic review and meta-analysis.

22 BANWELL, Foot orthoses for adults with flexible pes planus.

23 NEAL, Foot posture as a risk factor for lower limb overuse injury: A systematic review and meta-analysis.

24 VAN GENT, Incidence and determinants of lower extremity running injuries in long distance runners. See also VAN DER WORP, Injuries in runners: a systematic review on risk factors and sex differences. See also NEAL, Foot posture as a risk factor for lower limb overuse injury: A systematic review and meta-analysis.

25 KELLY, L.A.; CRESSWELL, A. G.; RACINAIS, S; WHITELEY, R.; LICHTWARK, G., Intrinsic foot muscles have the capacity to control deformation of the longitudinal arch. *Journal of the Royal Society, Interface,* v. 11, n. 93, 20131188, 2014. ISSN 1742-5689.

26 MILLER, E. E.; WHITCOME, K. K.; LIEBERMAN, D. E.; NORTON, H. L.; DYER, R. E., The effect of minimal shoes on arch structure and intrinsic foot muscle strength. *Journal of Sport and Health Science,* v. 3, n. 2, pp. 74–85, 2014. ISSN 2095-2546.

27 MCPOIL THOMAS, G.; CORNWALL MARK, W. Relationship between static foot posture and foot mobility. *Journal of Foot and Ankle Research,* v. 4, n. 1, p. 4, 2011. ISSN 1757-1146.

28 MCPOIL THOMAS, Relationship between static foot posture and foot mobility.

29 NIELSON, R. O.; BUIST, I.; PARNER, E. T.; NOHR, E. A.; SORENSEN, H.; LIND, M.; RASMUSSEN, S., Foot pronation is not associated with increased injury risk in novice runners wearing a neutral shoe: a 1-year prospective cohort study. *Br J Sports Med,* v. 48, n. 6, pp. 440–7, Mar 2014. ISSN 1473-0480. See also RICHARDS, C. E.; MAGIN, P. J.; CALLISTER, R., Is your prescription of distance running shoes evidence-based? *Br J Sports Med,* v. 43, n. 3, pp. 159–62, Mar 2009. ISSN 1473-0480.

30 LUCAS, R.; CORNWALL, M., Influence of foot posture on the functioning of the windlass mechanism. *Foot (Edinb),* v. 30, pp. 38–42, Mar 2017. ISSN 1532-2963.

31 KARANDIKAR, N.; VARGAS, O. O., Kinetic chains: a review of the concept and its clinical applications. *Pm&R,* v. 3, n. 8, pp. 739–45, Aug 2011. ISSN 1934-1482.

32 DAVIS, I. S.; RICE, H. M.; WEARING, S. C., Why forefoot striking in minimal shoes might positively change the course of running injuries. *Journal of Sport and Health Science,* v. 6, n. 2, pp. 154–61, 2017. ISSN 2095-2546.

33 DAOUD, A. I.; GEISSLER, G. J.; WANG, F.; SARETSKY, J.; DAOUD, Y. A.; LIEBERMAN, D. E., Foot strike and injury rates in endurance runners: a retrospective study. *Med Sci Sports Exerc,* v. 44, n. 7, pp. 1325–34, Jul 2012. ISSN 1530-0315.

34 DAOUD, Foot strike and injury rates in endurance runners.

35 DAOUD, Foot strike and injury rates in endurance runners.

36 LIEBERMAN, D. E.; VENKADESAN, M.; WERBEL, W. A.; DAOUD, A. I.; D'ANDREA, S.; DAVIS, I. S.; MANG'ENI, R. O.; PITSILADIS, Y., Foot

strike patterns and collision forces in habitually barefoot versus shod runners. *Nature,* v. 463, n. 7280, pp. 531–5, Jan 2010. ISSN 1476-4687.

37   DAVIS, Why forefoot striking in minimal shoes might positively change the course of running injuries. See also BOYER, E. R.; DERRICK, T. R., Select injury-related variables are affected by stride length and foot strike style during running. *Am J Sports Med,* v. 43, n. 9, pp. 2310–7, Sep 2015. ISSN 1552-3365. See also WARR, B. J.; FELLIN, R. E.; SAUER, S. G.; GOSS, D. L.; FRYKMAN, P. N.; SEAY, J. F., Characterization of Foot-Strike Patterns: Lack of an Association with Injuries or Performance in Soldiers. *Mil Med,* v. 180, n. 7, pp. 830–4, Jul 2015. ISSN 1930-613X. See also KASMER, M. E.; LIU, X. C.; ROBERTS, K. G.; VALADAO, J. M., Foot-strike pattern and performance in a marathon. *Int J Sports Physiol Perform,* v. 8, n. 3, p. 286–92, May 2013. ISSN 1555-0265. See also Anderson, L. M.; Bonanno, D. R.; Hart, H. F.; Barton, C. J., What are the Benefits and Risks Associated with Changing Foot Strike Pattern During Running? A Systematic Review and Meta-analysis of Injury, Running Economy, and Biomechanics. *Sports Medicine,* December 10 2019. ISSN 1179-2035.

38   DAVIS, Why forefoot striking in minimal shoes might positively change the course of running injuries.

39   DAVIS, Why forefoot striking in minimal shoes might positively change the course of running injuries.

40   DAVIS, Why forefoot striking in minimal shoes might positively change the course of running injuries. See also GRIER, T.; CANHAM-CHERVAK, M.; BUSHMAN, T.; ANDERSON, M.; NORTH, W.; JONES, B. H. Minimalist Running Shoes and Injury Risk Among United States Army Soldiers. *Am J Sports Med,* v. 44, n. 6, pp. 1439–46, Jun 2016. ISSN 1552-3365.

41   LIEBERMAN, Foot strike patterns and collision forces in habitually barefoot versus shod runners. See also MURPHY, K.; CURRY, E. J.; MATZKIN, E. G. Barefoot running: does it prevent injuries? *Sports Med,* v. 43, n. 11, p. 1131–8, Nov 2013. ISSN 1179-2035.

42   DAVIS, Why forefoot striking in minimal shoes might positively change the course of running injuries.

43   ANDERSON, What are the Benefits and Risks Associated with Changing Foot Strike Pattern During Running?.

44   LYGHT, M.; NOCKERTS, M.; KERNOZEK, T. W.; RAGAN, R., Effects of Foot Strike and Step Frequency on Achilles Tendon Stress During Running. *J Appl Biomech,* v. 32, n. 4, pp. 365–72, Aug 2016. ISSN 1543-2688.

45   BOYER, Select injury-related variables are affected by stride length and foot strike style during running. See also LYGHT, Effects of Foot Strike and Step Frequency on Achilles Tendon Stress During Running.

46   MURPHY, Barefoot running: does it prevent injuries?

47   MURPHY, Barefoot running: does it prevent injuries?

48   ALTMAN, Barefoot running: biomechanics and implications for running injuries.

49   ALTMAN, Barefoot running: biomechanics and implications for running injuries.

50   DAVIS, Why forefoot striking in minimal shoes might positively change the course of running injuries.

51 LYGHT, M.; NOCKERTS, M.; KERNOZEK, T. W.; RAGAN, R., Effects of Foot Strike and Step Frequency on Achilles Tendon Stress During Running. J Appl Biomech, v. 32, n. 4, pp. 365-72, Aug 2016. ISSN 1543-2688.

52 DAVIS, Why forefoot striking in minimal shoes might positively change the course of running injuries.

53 BOYER, Select injury-related variables are affected by stride length and foot strike style during running.

54 GERRARD, J. M.; BONANNO, D. R., Increasing preferred step rate during running reduces plantar pressures. Scand J Med Sci Sports, v. 28, n. 1, pp. 144-51, Jan 2018. ISSN 1600-0838. See also ALLEN, D. J.; HEISLER, H.; MOONEY, J.; KRING, R., The Effect of Step Rate Manipulation on Foot Strike of Long Distance Runners. Int J Sports Phys Ther, v. 11, n. 1, pp. 54-63, Feb 2016. ISSN 2159-2896.

55 HEIDERSCHEIT, B. C.; CHUMANOV, E. S.; MICHALSKI, M. P.; WILLE, C. M.; RYAN, M. B., Effects of step rate manipulation on joint mechanics during running. Med Sci Sports Exerc, v. 43, n. 2, pp. 296-302, Feb 2011. ISSN 1530-0315.

56 ZIMMERMANN, W. O.; BAKKER, E. W. P., Reducing vertical ground reaction forces: The relative importance of three gait retraining cues. Clinical Biomechanics, v. 69, pp. 16-20, 2019. ISSN 0268-0033.

57 HEIDERSCHEIT, Effects of step rate manipulation on joint mechanics during running.

58 HEIDERSCHEIT, Effects of step rate manipulation on joint mechanics during running.

59 DAVIS, Why forefoot striking in minimal shoes might positively change the course of running injuries.

60 LYGHT, Effects of Foot Strike and Step Frequency on Achilles Tendon Stress During Running.

61 DAVIS, Why forefoot striking in minimal shoes might positively change the course of running injuries.

62 DAVIS, Why forefoot striking in minimal shoes might positively change the course of running injuries. See also PERL, D. P.; DAOUD, A. I.; LIEBERMAN, D. E., Effects of footwear and strike type on running economy. Med Sci Sports Exerc, v. 44, n. 7, pp. 1335-43, Jul 2012. ISSN 1530-0315.

63 PERL, Effects of footwear and strike type on running economy.

64 HASEGAWA, H.; YAMAUCHI, T.; KRAEMER, W. J., Foot strike patterns of runners at the 15-km point during an elite-level half marathon. J Strength Cond Res, v. 21, n. 3, pp. 888-93, Aug 2007. ISSN 1064-8011.

65 LARSON, P.; HIGGINS, E.; KAMINSKI, J.; DECKER, T.; PREBLE, J.; LYONS, D.; McINTYRE, K.; NORMILE, A., Foot strike patterns of recreational and sub-elite runners in a long-distance road race. J Sports Sci, v. 29, n. 15, pp. 1665-73, Dec 2011. ISSN 1466-447X.

66 LARSON, Foot strike patterns of recreational and sub-elite runners in a long-distance road race.

67 WERD, M. B., KNIGHT, E. LESLIE, LANGER, PAUL R., Athletic Footwear & Orthoses in Sports Medicine. Evolution of Athletic Footwear. SUBOTNICK, S. I.: Springer International Publishing 2017.

68 VAN DER WORP, Do runners who suffer injuries have higher vertical ground reaction forces than those who remain injury-free?.

69 NIELSON, Foot pronation is not associated with increased injury risk in novice runners wearing a neutral shoe: a 1-year prospective cohort study. See also RICHARDSIs your prescription of distance running shoes evidence-based?

70 CHEUNG, R. T.; NGAI, S. P., Effects of footwear on running economy in distance runners: A meta-analytical review. *J Sci Med Sport*, v. 19, n. 3, pp. 260–6, Mar 2016. ISSN 1878-1861.

71 WERD, M. B., KNIGHT, E. LESLIE, LANGER, PAUL R., *Athletic Footwear & Orthoses in Sports Medicine. Evolution of Athletic Footwear.* SUBOTNICK, S. I.: Springer International Publishing 2017.

72 RICHARDS, Is your prescription of distance running shoes evidence-based?.

73 KULMALA, J. P.; KISONEN, J.; NURMINEN, J.; AVELA, J., Running in highly cushioned shoes increases leg stiffness and amplifies impact loading. *Sci Rep*, v. 8, n. 1, p. 174-196, Nov 2018. ISSN 2045-2322.

74 NIGG, B. M.; BALTICH, J.; HOERZER, S.; ENDERS, H., Running shoes and running injuries: mythbusting and a proposal for two new paradigms: 'preferred movement path' and 'comfort filter'. *Br J Sports Med*, v. 49, n. 20, p. 1290–4, Oct 2015. ISSN 1473-0480.

75 WERD, *Athletic Footwear & Orthoses in Sports Medicine.*

76 WERD, *Athletic Footwear & Orthoses in Sports Medicine.*

77 RICHARDS, Is your prescription of distance running shoes evidence-based?. See also NIGG, B. M.; BALTICH, J.; HOERZER, S.; ENDERS, H., Running shoes and running injuries: mythbusting and a proposal for two new paradigms: 'preferred movement path' and 'comfort filter'. *Br J Sports Med*, v. 49, n. 20, pp. 1290–4, Oct 2015. ISSN 1473-0480. See also NIGG, B. M.; VIENNEAU, J.; SMITH, A. C.; TRUDEAU, M. B.; MOHR, M.; NIGG, S. R., The Preferred Movement Path Paradigm: Influence of Running Shoes on Joint Movement. *Med Sci Sports Exerc*, v. 49, n. 8, pp. 1641–8, Aug 2017. ISSN 1530-0315.

78 RICHARDS, Is your prescription of distance running shoes evidence-based?. See also NIGG, Running shoes and running injuries: mythbusting and a proposal for two new paradigms: 'preferred movement path' and 'comfort filter'. See also NIGG, The Preferred Movement Path Paradigm: Influence of Running Shoes on Joint Movement.

79 NIGG, Running shoes and running injuries: mythbusting and a proposal for two new paradigms: 'preferred movement path' and 'comfort filter'.

80 NIGG, Running shoes and running injuries: mythbusting and a proposal for two new paradigms: 'preferred movement path' and 'comfort filter'.

81 NIGG, Running shoes and running injuries: mythbusting and a proposal for two new paradigms: 'preferred movement path' and 'comfort filter', p. 4

82 NIGG, Running shoes and running injuries: mythbusting and a proposal for two new paradigms: 'preferred movement path' and 'comfort filter'.

83 LIEBERMAN, Foot strike patterns and collision forces in habitually barefoot versus shod runners. See also NICHOLAS, B. H.; IAN, J. W.; DANIEL, E. L., Foot strength and stiffness are related to footwear use in a comparison of minimally- vs. conventionally-shod populations. *Scientific Reports*, v. 8, n. 1, pp. 1–12, 2018. ISSN 2045-2322.

84   MCDOUGALL, C., Born to Run: A hidden tribe, superathletes, and the greatest race the world has never seen. New York.: Knopf, 2009. ISBN 13 9781861978776.

85   JENKINS, D. W.; CAUTHON, D. J., Barefoot running claims and controversies: a review of the literature. *J Am Podiatr Med Assoc*, v. 101, n. 3, pp. 231–46, May-Jun 2011. ISSN 1930-8264.

86   ESCULIER, J. F.; DUBOIS, B.; DIONNE, C. E.; LEBLOND, J.; ROY, J. S., A consensus definition and rating scale for minimalist shoes. *J Foot Ankle Res*, v. 8, p. 42, 2015. ISSN 1757-1146.

87   MALISOUX, L.; CHAMBON, N.; URHAUSEN, A.; THEISEN, D. Influence of the Heel-to-Toe Drop of Standard Cushioned Running Shoes on Injury Risk in Leisure-Time Runners: A Randomized Controlled Trial With 6-Month Follow-up. *Am J Sports Med*, v. 44, n. 11, p. 2933–40, Nov 2016. ISSN 1552-3365.

88   ALTMAN, Barefoot running: biomechanics and implications for running injuries.

89   ALTMAN, Barefoot running: biomechanics and implications for running injuries.

90   DAVIS, Why forefoot striking in minimal shoes might positively change the course of running injuries.

91   TAM, N.; ASTEPHEN WILSON, J. L.; NOAKES, T. D.; TUCKER, R., Barefoot running: an evaluation of current hypothesis, future research and clinical applications. *Br J Sports Med*, v. 48, n. 5, pp. 349–55, Mar 2014. ISSN 1473-0480.

92   DAVIS, Why forefoot striking in minimal shoes might positively change the course of running injuries. See also LIEBERMAN, Foot strike patterns and collision forces in habitually barefoot versus shod runners. See also GRIER, Minimalist Running Shoes and Injury Risk Among United States Army Soldiers.

93   LIEBERMAN, Foot strike patterns and collision forces in habitually barefoot versus shod runners. See also MURPHY, Barefoot running: does it prevent injuries?

94   BONACCI, Running in a minimalist and lightweight shoe is not the same as running barefoot: a biomechanical study.

95   ROBBINS, S. E.; HANNA, A. M., Running-related injury prevention through barefoot adaptations. *Medicine and Science in Sports and Exercise*, v. 19, n. 2, pp. 148–56, 1987. ISSN 0195-9131.

96   MILLER, The effect of minimal shoes on arch structure and intrinsic foot muscle strength.

97   FREDERICK, E. C.; DANIELS, J. R.; HAYES, J. W., The effect of shoe weight on the aerobic demands of running. *Current Topics in Sports Medicine*, pp. 616–25, 1984.

98   SQUADRONE, R.; GALLOZZI, C. Biomechanical and physiological comparison of barefoot and two shod conditions in experienced barefoot runners. *J Sports Med Phys Fitness*, v. 49, n. 1, p. 6–13, Mar 2009. ISSN 0022-4707.

99   CHEUNG, Effects of footwear on running economy in distance runners: A meta-analytical review.

100 ALTMAN, Barefoot running: biomechanics and implications for running injuries.

101 HALL, J. P.; BARTON, C.; JONES, P. R.; MORRISSEY, D., The biomechanical differences between barefoot and shod distance running: a systematic review and preliminary meta-analysis. *Sports Med*, v. 43, n. 12, pp. 1335-53, Dec 2013. ISSN 1179-2035.

102 FULLER, J. T.; THEWLIS, D.; BUCKLEY, J. D.; BROWN, N. A.; HAMILL, J.; TSIROS, M. D., Body Mass and Weekly Training Distance Influence the Pain and Injuries Experienced by Runners Using Minimalist Shoes: A Randomized Controlled Trial. *Am J Sports Med*, v. 45, n. 5, pp. 1162-70, Apr 2017. ISSN 1552-3365.

103 SERRAO, J. C., Does 'transition shoe' promote an intermediate biomechanical condition compared to running in conventional shoe and in reduced protection condition? *Gait Posture*, v. 46, pp. 142-6, May 2016. ISSN 1879-2219.

104 www.hokaoneone.com/brand-origins.html. Accessed: 6th July 2019.

105 www.triathlete.com/2018/10/gear-tech/kona-2018-running-shoe-count-hoka-reigns-again_336635. Kona 2018 Running Shoe Count: Hoka Reigns Again. 2018. Accessed: 6th July 2019.

106 KULMALA, Running in highly cushioned shoes increases leg stiffness and amplifies impact loading.

107 CHAN, Z. Y. S.; AU, I. P. H.; LAU, F. O. Y.; CHING, E. C. K.; ZHANG, J. H.; CHEUNG, R. T. H., Does maximalist footwear lower impact loading during level ground and downhill running? *Eur J Sport Sci*, v. 18, n. 8, pp. 1083-9, Sep 2018. ISSN 1536-7290.

108 KULMALA, Running in highly cushioned shoes increases leg stiffness and amplifies impact loading.

109 SOBHANI, S.; VAN DEN HEUVEL, E.; BREDEWEG, S.; KLUITENBERG, B.; POSTEMA, K.; HIJMANS, J. M.; DEKKER, R., Effect of rocker shoes on plantar pressure pattern in healthy female runners. *Gait Posture*, v. 39, n. 3, pp. 920-5, Mar 2014. ISSN 1879-2219.

110 LMEIDA, What are the main running-related musculoskeletal injuries? A systematic review.

111 SOBHANI, S.; ZWERVER, J.; VAN DEN HEUVEL, E.; POSTEMA, K., DEKKER, R.; HIJMANS, J. M., Rocker shoes reduce Achilles tendon load in running and walking in patients with chronic Achilles tendinopathy. *J Sci Med Sport*, v. 18, n. 2, pp. 133-8, Mar 2015. ISSN 1878-1861.

112 SOBHANI, S.; VAN DEN HEUVEL, E. R.; DEKKER, R.; POSTEMA, K.; KLUITENBERG, B.; BREDEWEG, S. W.; HIJMANS, J. M., Biomechanics of running with rocker shoes. *J Sci Med Sport*, v. 20, n. 1, pp. 38-44, Jan 2017. ISSN 1878-1861.

113 NIGG, Running shoes and running injuries: mythbusting and a proposal for two new paradigms: 'preferred movement path' and 'comfort filter'.

114 NAPIER, C.; WILLY, R. W., Logical fallacies in the running shoe debate: let the evidence guide prescription. *British Journal of Sports Medicine*, v. 52, n. 24, pp. 1552-1553, 2018. ISSN 0306-3674.

115 NIGG, Running shoes and running injuries: mythbusting and a proposal for two new paradigms: 'preferred movement path' and 'comfort filter'. See also Taunton, J.E., Ryan, M.B., Clement, D.B., et al., A prospective study of running injuries: the Vancouver Sun Run 'In Training' clinics, *Br J Sports Med* 2003;**37**:239-44. doi:10.1136/bjsm.37.3.239; Van Middelkoop, M., Kolkman, J., Van Ochten, J., et al., Prevalence and incidence of lower extremity injuries in male marathon runners, Scand J Med Sci Sports 2008;18:140-4. doi:10.1111/j.1600-0838.2007.00683.x; and Buist, I., Bredeweg, S.W., Lemmink, K.A., et al., Predictors of running-related injuries in novice runners enrolled in a systematic training program: a prospective cohort study, Am J Sports Med 2010;38:273-80. doi:10.1177/036354650934798.

116 NIGG, Running shoes and running injuries: mythbusting and a proposal for two new paradigms: 'preferred movement path' and 'comfort filter'.

117 YAMATO, T. P.; SARAGIOTTO, B. T.; LOPES, A. D., A consensus definition of running-related injury in recreational runners: a modified Delphi approach. *J Orthop Sports Phys Ther,* v. 45, n. 5, pp. 375-80, May 2015. ISSN 1938-1344.

118 NIGG, Running shoes and running injuries: mythbusting and a proposal for two new paradigms: 'preferred movement path' and 'comfort filter'.

119 NIGG, Running shoes and running injuries: mythbusting and a proposal for two new paradigms: 'preferred movement path' and 'comfort filter'.

120 FREDERICK, E. C.; DANIELS, J. R.; HAYES, J. W., The effect of shoe weight on the aerobic demands of running. *Current Topics in Sports Medicine,* pp. 616-25, 1984.

121 NIGG, Running shoes and running injuries: mythbusting and a proposal for two new paradigms: 'preferred movement path' and 'comfort filter'.

122 PERL, D. P.; DAOUD, A. I.; LIEBERMAN, D. E., Effects of footwear and strike type on running economy. *Med Sci Sports Exerc,* v. 44, n. 7, pp. 1335-43, Jul 2012. ISSN 1530-0315.

123 FULLER, J. T.; THEWLIS, D.; TSIROS, M. D.; BROWN, N. A. T.; BUCKLEY, J. D., Effects of a minimalist shoe on running economy and 5-km running performance. *Journal of Sports Sciences,* v. 34, n. 18, pp. 1740-5, 2016. ISSN 0264-0414.

124 TUNG, K. D.; FRANZ, J. R.; KRAM, R., A test of the metabolic cost of cushioning hypothesis during unshod and shod running. *Medicine and science in sports and exercise,* v. 46, n. 2, p. 324, 2014. ISSN 0195-9131.

125 TUNG, A test of the metabolic cost of cushioning hypothesis during unshod and shod running.

126 WOROBETS, J; WANNOP, J. W.; TOMARAS, E.; STEFANYSHYN, D., Softer and more resilient running shoe cushioning properties enhance running economy. Footwear Science, v. 6, n. 3, pp. 147-53, 2014. ISSN 1942-4280.

127 FULLER, J. T.; BELLENGER, C.; THEWLIS, D.; TSIROS, M. D.; BUCKLEY, J. D., The Effect of Footwear on Running Performance and Running Economy in Distance Runners. *Sports Medicine,* Cham, v. 45, n. 3, pp. 411-22, 2015. ISSN 0112-1642.

128 FULLER, The Effect of Footwear on Running Performance and Running Economy in Distance Runners.

129 HOOGKAMER, W.; KIPP, S.; FRANK, J. H.; FARINA, E. M.; LUO, G.; KRAM, R., A Comparison of the Energetic Cost of Running in Marathon Racing Shoes. *Sports Med*, v. 48, n. 4, pp. 1009-19, April 2018. ISSN 1179-2035.

130 BURNS, G. T.; TAM, N., Is it the shoes? A simple proposal for regulating footwear in road running. *British Journal of Sports Medicine*, 2019. ISSN 0306-3674.

131 HOOGKAMER, A Comparison of the Energetic Cost of Running in Marathon Racing Shoes.

132 HOOGKAMER, A Comparison of the Energetic Cost of Running in Marathon Racing Shoes.

133 VAN DER WORP, Injuries in runners: a systematic review on risk factors and sex differences.

134 SULLIVAN, J.; BURNS, J.; ADAMS, R.; PAPPAS, E.; CROSBIE, J., Musculoskeletal and activity-related factors associated with plantar heel pain. *Foot Ankle Int*, v. 36, n. 1, pp. 37-45, Jan 2015. ISSN 1944-7876.

135 LATEY, P. J.; BURNS, J.; HILLER, C. E.; NIGHTINGALE, E. J., Relationship between foot pain, muscle strength and size: a systematic review. *Physiotherapy*, v. 103, n. 1, pp. 13-20, Mar 2017. ISSN 1873-1465.

136 HUFFER, D.; HING, W.; NEWTON, R.; CLAIR, M., Strength training for plantar fasciitis and the intrinsic foot musculature: A systematic review. *Phys Ther Sport*, v. 24, pp. 44-52, Mar 2017. ISSN 1873-1600.

137 HUFFER, Strength training for plantar fasciitis and the intrinsic foot musculature: A systematic review.

138 KELLY, Intrinsic foot muscles have the capacity to control deformation of the longitudinal arch.

139 KELLY, Intrinsic foot muscles have the capacity to control deformation of the longitudinal arch.

140 MILLER, E. E.; WHITCOME, K. K.; LIEBERMAN, D. E.; NORTON, H. L.; DYER, R. E., The effect of minimal shoes on arch structure and intrinsic foot muscle strength. *Journal of Sport and Health Science*, v. 3, n. 2, pp. 74-85, 2014. ISSN 2095-2546.

141 LIEBERMAN, D. E.; VENKADESAN, M.; WERBEL, W. A.; DAOUD, A. I.; D'ANDREA, S.; DAVIS, I. S.; MANG'ENI, R. O.; PITSILADIS, Y., Foot strike patterns and collision forces in habitually barefoot versus shod runners. *Nature*, v. 463, n. 7280, pp. 531-5, Jan 2010. ISSN 1476-4687.

142 NAPIER, C.; WILLY, R. W., Logical fallacies in the running shoe debate: let the evidence guide prescription. *British Journal of Sports Medicine*, v. 52, n. 24, 2018. ISSN 0306-3674.

143 NIGG, Running shoes and running injuries: mythbusting and a proposal for two new paradigms: 'preferred movement path' and 'comfort filter'.

144 WERD, M. B., KNIGHT, E. LESLIE, LANGER, PAUL R., *Athletic Footwear & Orthoses in Sports Medicine. Evolution of Athletic Footwear.* SUBOTNICK, S. I.: Springer International Publishing 2017.

145 WERD, *Athletic Footwear & Orthoses in Sports Medicine. Evolution of Athletic Footwear.*

146 WERD, *Athletic Footwear & Orthoses in Sports Medicine. Evolution of Athletic Footwear.*

147   WERD, *Athletic Footwear & Orthoses in Sports Medicine. Evolution of Athletic Footwear.*

148   WERD, *Athletic Footwear & Orthoses in Sports Medicine. Evolution of Athletic Footwear.*

149   WERD, *Athletic Footwear & Orthoses in Sports Medicine. Evolution of Athletic Footwear.*

150   WERD, *Athletic Footwear & Orthoses in Sports Medicine. Evolution of Athletic Footwear.*

151   MALISOUX, L.; RAMESH, J.; MANN, R.; SEIL, R.; URHAUSEN, A.; THEISEN, D., Can parallel use of different running shoes decrease running-related injury risk? *Scandinavian Journal of Medicine & Science in Sports*, v. 25, n. 1, pp. 110–15, 2015. ISSN 0905-7188.

152   RETHNAM, U.; MAKWANA, N., Are old running shoes detrimental to your feet? A pedobarographic study. *BMC Research Notes*, London, v. 4, n. 1, pp. 307, 2011. ISSN 1756-0500.

153   COOK, S. D.; KESTER, M. A.; BRUNET, M. E., Shock absorption characteristics of running shoes. *Am J Sports Med*, v. 13, n. 4, pp. 248–53, 1985 Jul-Aug 1985. ISSN 0363-5465.

154   WANG, L.; XIAN L, J.; HONG, Y.; HE ZHOU, J., Changes in heel cushioning characteristics of running shoes with running mileage. *Footwear Science*, v. 2, n. 3, pp. 141–7, 2010. ISSN 1942-4280. See also KONG, P. W.; CANDELARIA, N. G.; SMITH, D. R., Running in new and worn shoes: a comparison of three types of cushioning footwear. *British Journal of Sports Medicine*, v. 43, n. 10, p. 745, 2009. ISSN 0306-3674.

155   DORLAND, W. A. N., Dorland's Illustrated Medical Dictionary: Saunders 2003. ISBN 0-7216-0146-4.

156   HADJIDAKIS, D. J.; ANDROULAKIS, I. I., Bone remodeling. *Ann N Y Acad Sci*, v. 1092, pp. 385–96, Dec 2006. ISSN 0077-8923.

157   KIEL, J., K. K., *Stress Reaction and Fractures. In: StatPearls [Internet].*: Treasure Island (FL): StatPearls Publishing; 2018 Jan-. [Updated 2018 Oct 27].

158   KIEL, *Stress Reaction and Fractures.*

159   NOSE-OGURA, S.; HARADA, M.; HIRAIKE, O.; OSUGA, Y.; FUJII, T., Management of the female athlete triad. *J Obstet Gynaecol Res*, Apr 2018. ISSN 1447-0756.

160   NOSE-OGURA, Management of the female athlete triad.

161   KIEL, *Stress Reaction and Fractures.*

162   KIEL, *Stress Reaction and Fractures.*

163   KIEL, *Stress Reaction and Fractures.*

164   RODOLA, C. G.; CAPPELLO, F.; MARCIANO, V.; FRANCAVILLA, C.; MONTALLBANO, A.; FARINA LIPARI, E.; PALMA, A., The synovial joints of the human foot. *Ital J Anat Embryol*, v. 112, n. 2, pp. 61–80, Apr-Jun 2007. ISSN 1122-6714 (Print). 1122-6714.

165   RALPHS, J. R.; BENJAMIN, M., The joint capsule: structure, composition, ageing and disease. *J Anat*, v. 184 (Pt 3), pp. 503–9, Jun 1994. ISSN 0021-8782.

166   RALPHS, The joint capsule: structure, composition, ageing and disease.

167   RALPHS, The joint capsule: structure, composition, ageing and disease.

168 SOPHIA FOX, A. J.; BEDI, A.; RODEO, S. A., The basic science of articular cartilage: structure, composition, and function. *Sports Health*, v. 1, n. 6, pp. 461–8, Nov 2009. ISSN 1941-7381.

169 SOPHIA FOX, The basic science of articular cartilage: structure, composition, and function.

170 MCSWEENEY, S., First Metatarsophalangeal Joint Osteoarthritis - A clinical review. *Journal of Novel Physiotherapies*, v. 6, p. 293, 2016.

171 MCSWEENEY, First Metatarsophalangeal Joint Osteoarthritis.

172 MCSWEENEY, First Metatarsophalangeal Joint Osteoarthritis.

173 MCSWEENEY, First Metatarsophalangeal Joint Osteoarthritis.

174 HAUSER, R. A.; DOLAN, E. E.; PHILLIPS, H. J.; NEWLIN, A.C.; MOORE, R.E.; WOLDIN, B.A. Ligament Injury and Healing: A Review of Current Clinical Diagnostics and Therapeutics. *The Open Rehabilitation Journal*, v. 6, p. 1–20, 2013.

175 HAUSER, Ligament Injury and Healing: A Review of Current Clinical Diagnostics and Therapeutics.

176 HAUSER, Ligament Injury and Healing: A Review of Current Clinical Diagnostics and Therapeutics.

177 BARAVARIAN, B.; REDKAR, A., Expert insights to treating plantar plate tears. *Podiatry Today*, v. 29, n. 3, pp. 60–3, 2016.

178 DELAND, J. T.; LEE, K. T.; SOBEL, M.; DICARLO, E. F., Anatomy of the plantar plate and its attachments in the lesser metatarsal phalangeal joint. *Foot Ankle Int*, v. 16, n. 8, pp. 480–6, Aug 1995. ISSN 1071-1007.

179 KIRBY, K., Understanding the Biomechanics of Plantar Plate Injuries. *Podiatry Today*, v. 30, n. 4, pp. 30–9, 2017.

180 BARAVARIAN, Expert insights to treating plantar plate tears.

181 BARAVARIAN, Expert insights to treating plantar plate tears.

182 BOELCH, S. P.; JANSEN, H.; MEFFERT, R. H.; FREY, S. P., Six Sesamoid Bones on Both Feet: Report of a Rare Case. *J Clin Diagn Res*, v. 9, n. 8, pp. RD04–5, Aug 2015. ISSN 2249-782X.

183 BOELCH, Six Sesamoid Bones on Both Feet: Report of a Rare Case.

184 JEFFREY, A. R., A comprehensive guide to reviving the sick sesamoid. *Podiatry Today*, v. 29, n. 4, pp. 68–71, 2016.

185 JEFFREY, A comprehensive guide to reviving the sick sesamoid.

186 JEFFREY, A comprehensive guide to reviving the sick sesamoid.

187 NOAKES, T. D. *Lore of Running*. 4th. Oxford University Press Southern Africa, 2001. ISBN: 9780873229593.

188 TALBOT, J.; MAVES, L., Skeletal muscle fiber type: using insights from muscle developmental biology to dissect targets for susceptibility and resistance to muscle disease. *Wiley Interdiscip Rev Dev Biol*, v. 5, n. 4, pp. 518–34, 07 2016. ISSN 1759-7692.

189 TALBOT, Skeletal muscle fiber type: using insights from muscle developmental biology to dissect targets for susceptibility and resistance to muscle disease.

190 NOAKES, *Lore of Running*.

191 SIMONEAU, J. A.; BOUCHARD, C., Genetic determinism of fiber type proportion in human skeletal muscle. *FASEB J*, v. 9, n. 11, pp. 1091–5, Aug 1995. ISSN 0892-6638.

192 TALBOT, Skeletal muscle fiber type: using insights from muscle developmental biology to dissect targets for susceptibility and resistance to muscle disease.

193 TALBOT, Skeletal muscle fiber type: using insights from muscle developmental biology to dissect targets for susceptibility and resistance to muscle disease.

194 TALBOT, Skeletal muscle fiber type: using insights from muscle developmental biology to dissect targets for susceptibility and resistance to muscle disease.

195 NOAKES, *Lore of Running.*

196 NOAKES, *Lore of Running.*

197 HOLLOSZY, J. O., Adaptation of skeletal muscle to endurance exercise. *Med Sci Sports*, v. 7, n. 3, pp. 155–64, 1975. ISSN 0025-7990.

198 MYBURGH, K.H.; WESTON, A.R., The human endurance athlete: heterogeneity and adaptability of selected exercise and skeletal muscle characteristics. *South African Journal of Zoology*, v. 33, n. 2, pp. 129–40, 1998.

199 GALLO, R. A.; PLAKKE, M.; SILVIS, M. L., Common leg injuries of long-distance runners: anatomical and biomechanical approach. *Sports Health*, v. 4, n. 6, pp. 485–95, Nov 2012. ISSN 1941-0921.

200 GALLO, Common leg injuries of long-distance runners: anatomical and biomechanical approach.

201 GLENN, N. O.; HENRY, C. A., How muscle contraction strengthens tendons. *Elife*, v. 8, pp. 1-3, Jan 2019. ISSN 2050-084X.

202 KANNUS, P., Structure of the tendon connective tissue. *Scand J Med Sci Sports*, v. 10, n. 6, pp. 312–20, Dec 2000. ISSN 0905-7188.

203 BORDONI, B.; VARACALLO, M., Anatomy, Tendons: StatPearls Publishing LLC. 2018.

204 BORDONI, Tendons.

205 DORAL, M. N.; ALAM, M.; BOZKURT, M.; TURHAN, E.; ATAY, O. A.; DONMEZ, G.; MAFFULLI, N., Functional anatomy of the Achilles tendon. *Knee Surg Sports Traumatol Arthrosc*, v. 18, n. 5, pp. 638–43, May 2010. ISSN 1433-7347.

206 ALMEIDA, M. O.; DAVIS, I. S.; LOPES, A. D., What are the main running-related musculoskeletal injuries? A Systematic Review. *Sports Med*, v. 42, n. 10, pp. 891–905, Oct 2012. ISSN 1179-2035.

207 LI, H. Y.; HUA, Y. H., Achilles Tendinopathy: Current Concepts about the Basic Science and Clinical Treatments. *Biomed Res Int*, v. 2016, pp. 6492597, pp. 1-10, 2016. ISSN 2314-6141.

208 LI, Achilles Tendinopathy: Current Concepts about the Basic Science and Clinical Treatments.

209 ROCHE, A. J.; CALDER, J. D., Achilles tendinopathy: A review of the current concepts of treatment. *Bone Joint J*, v. 95-B, n. 10, pp. 1299–307, Oct 2013. ISSN 2049-4408.

210 LI, Achilles Tendinopathy: Current Concepts about the Basic Science and Clinical Treatments.

211 IRWIN, T. A., Current concepts review: insertional Achilles tendinopathy. *Foot Ankle Int*, v. 31, n. 10, p. 933–9, Oct 2010. ISSN 1071-1007.

212 STECCO, C.; MACCHI, V.; PORZIONATO, A.; DUPARC, F.; DE CARO, R., The fascia: the forgotten structure. *Ital J Anat Embryol,* v. 116, n. 3, pp. 127–38, 2011. ISSN 1122-6714.

213 STECCO, The fascia: the forgotten structure.

214 STECCO, The fascia: the forgotten structure.

215 BOURNE, M.; VARACALLO, M., Anatomy, Bony Pelvis and Lower Limb, Foot Fascia. In: (Ed.). *StatPearls.* Treasure Island (FL): StatPearls Publishing LLC., 2018.

216 CHEN, D. W.; LI, B.; AUBEELUCK, A.; YANG, Y. F.; HUANG, Y. G.; ZHOU, J. Q.; YU, G. R. Anatomy and biomechanical properties of the plantar aponeurosis: a cadaveric study. *PLoS ONE,* v. 9, n. 1, p. e84347, 2014. ISSN 1932-6203.

217 CHEN, Anatomy and biomechanical properties of the plantar aponeurosis: a cadaveric study.

218 CHEN, Anatomy and biomechanical properties of the plantar aponeurosis: a cadaveric study.

219 PETRAGLIA, F.; RAMAZZINA, I.; COSTANTINO, C., Plantar fasciitis in athletes: diagnostic and treatment strategies. A systematic review. *Muscles Ligaments Tendons J,* v. 7, n. 1, pp. 107–118, 2017 Jan-Mar 2017. ISSN 2240-4554.

220 LANDORF, K. B., Plantar heel pain and plantar fasciitis. *BMJ Clin Evid,* v. 2015, Nov 2015. ISSN 1752-8526.

221 MONTEAGUDO, M.; DE ALBORNOZ, P. M.; GUTIERREZ, B.; TABUENCA, J.; ALVAREZ, I., Plantar fasciopathy: A current concepts review. *EFORT Open Rev,* v. 3, n. 8, pp. 485–93, Aug 2018. ISSN 2058-5241 (Print).

222 MONTEAGUDO, Plantar fasciopathy: A current concepts review.

223 Almeida, What are the main running-related musculoskeletal injuries? A Systematic Review.

224 PETRAGLIA, Plantar fasciitis in athletes: diagnostic and treatment strategies.

225 PEKALA, P. A.; HENRY, B. M.; PEKALA, J. R.; PISKA, K.; TOMASZEWSKI, K. A., The Achilles tendon and the retrocalcaneal bursa: An anatomical and radiological study. *Bone Joint Res,* v. 6, n. 7, pp. 446–51, Jul 2017. ISSN 2046-3758.

226 PEKALA, The Achilles tendon and the retrocalcaneal bursa: An anatomical and radiological study.

227 PEKALA, The Achilles tendon and the retrocalcaneal bursa: An anatomical and radiological study.

228 SCHEPSIS, A. A.; JONES, H.; HAAS, A. L., Achilles tendon disorders in athletes. *Am J Sports Med,* v. 30, n. 2, pp. 287–305, 2002 Mar-Apr 2002. ISSN 0363-5465.

229 MARIEB, E. N.; HOEHN, K., *Human Anatomy & Physiology.* 8th. San Francisco, CA, USA: Pearson Benjamin Cummings, 2010. ISBN: 978-0-321-60261-9.

230 MARIEB, *Human Anatomy & Physiology.*

231 MARIEB, *Human Anatomy & Physiology.*

232 MARIEB, *Human Anatomy & Physiology.*

233 LORIMER, Neale's Disorders of the Foot: Diagnosis and Management.

234 WERD, *Athletic Footwear & Orthoses in Sports Medicine.*

235 WERD, *Athletic Footwear & Orthoses in Sports Medicine.*

236 JUNG, D.Y.; KOH, E.K.; KWON, O.Y., Effect of foot orthoses and short-foot exercise on the cross-sectional area of the abductor hallucis muscle in subjects with pes planus: a randomized controlled trial. *Journal of back and musculoskeletal rehabilitation,* v. 24, n. 4, p. 225, 2011. ISSN 1053-8127. See also MURLEY, G. S.; LANDORF, K. B.; MENZ, H. B., Do foot orthoses change lower limb muscle activity in flat-arched feet towards a pattern observed in normal-arched feet? *Clinical Biomechanics,* v. 25, n. 7, pp. 728–36, 2010. ISSN 0268-0033. See also MURLEY, G. S.; LANDORF, K. B.; MENZ, H. B.; BIRD, A. R., Effect of foot posture, foot orthoses and footwear on lower limb muscle activity during walking and running: A systematic review. *Gait & Posture,* v. 29, n. 2, pp. 172–87, 2009. ISSN 0966-6362.

237 MENZ, H. B., Foot orthoses: how much customisation is necessary? *Journal of foot and ankle research,* v. 2, n. 1, p. 23, 2009. ISSN 1757-1146.

www.ingramcontent.com/pod-product-compliance
Lightning Source LLC
Chambersburg PA
CBHW072019060426
42446CB00044B/2806